Union-Free Supervisor

Union-Free Supervisor

James L. Dougherty

GULF PUBLISHING COMPANY
Book Publishing Division: Houston

Union-Free Supervisor

ISBN 0-87201-882-2
Library of Congress Catalog Card No. 74-11836

Contents

Introduction   **ix**

Union & Company

1   **The Impact of Unionism**   **3**

The Supervisor's Challenge; Effect on the Company; National Labor Law; The Situation; The Seniority Principle; Job Narrowing; Reduction of Output; Equal Pay for Equal Work; Relinquishment of Management Rights; Effect on Employees; Effect on the Nation; Fair Employment Threatened; Effect on Supervisors; Conclusion

2   **How & Why a Union Organizes**   **20**

How the Union Campaigns; The Four Phases of Campaigning; The Exploratory Phase; The Sub Rosa Campaign; The Open Campaign—No Election Pending; The Pre-Election Phase; WHY the Union Campaigns; The Union Invests

3   **How the Company Defends**   **38**
    Long Range Program

Defensive Plans; The Long Range Program; The Business Climate; The Union; The Employee; Weeding Out Undesirables; The Work Environment; The Specific Preparations; Pay, Benefits and Work Practices; Wages; Health Plans; Pension Plans and Savings Plans; Seniority; Transfers and Assignments; Complaint Handling; Discipline; New

Ideas; Communications Training; Blocking Unwanted Communication; Conclusion

4   How the Company Defends   59
      Short Range Program

Organizing Problems; The New Work Scene; The New Employee Mix; Union Leadership; Management Action; The Plan; Decisions Needed: Sub Rosa Phase; Strategy; Fence Mending; Specific Preparations; Information Gathering; Training; Management Strategy Shift; The Open Campaign Phase; Open Campaign—Before NLRB Hearing; Training; Legal Counsel; Campaign Strategy; Open Campaign—Before Election Date is Firm; Communicating; Company Campaign Tone; Campaign Content; Open Campaign—After Election Date Known; The Post-Election Period; Conclusion; Central Figure

5   White Collars & Union-Free Pockets   75

Union Label for the White Collar?; The Genus White Collar; Professionals; Quasi-Unions; Clericals; Technicals; Sales People; What Company and Supervisor Do—Long Range; The Business Environment; The Union; The Employee; The Work Environment; The Specific Preparations; Pay, Benefits and Work Practices; Training-Communication; What Company and Supervisor Do—Short Range: The Union Message; The Employer Short Range Campaign; Pockets of Union-Free People; Company Action; Defending the Pocket—Long Range Plan; Defending the Pocket—Short Range

6   The Union Communicates Ideas   94

Emphasis on Face to Face; Different Strokes for Different Folks; Responsiveness the Key; The Most-Used Themes; How Can We? What to Expect; Look Out Below; Do You Have Troubles?; For Women Only; For Women Only—A Special Message on the Advantages of a Union Contract; Dignity of Man; Sign Up Fast!; Demand for Recognition; Dues; We Like Our Union; Get a Contract; Exploiting Weaknesses; 'Taint So; The Best People; Great Men Agree . . . Unions are Good—Are Superior's Workers Asking Too Much?

7   The Company Communicates Ideas   110

The Early Maneuvering; When the Election is Scheduled; Ill Effects of Unionism; Unrest and Discontent; Union Promises; Job Security; Loss of the Personal Touch; Worsen a Bad Financial Situation; Something to Lose; the Union Clique; Seniority of Union Representatives; The Strike Threat; Union Violence; Advantages of Dealing With the Company; The Infighting; "What do I have to lose?"; Final Campaign; The Captive Audience; The Supervisor as Crisis Communicator

Employee & Supervisor

8   The "New" Employee   137

A Different Worker; The New Environment; A Different Attitude; Work a Game?" Poor Performance and Morale; What Do They Want?; Motivator-Dissatisfier; The Motivators; The Dissatisfiers; Prescription; The Group; The New Breed

9   The New Supervision   152
Fresh Goals and Skills

The Importance of Attitude; Self Improvement; Areas of Skill; Training Factors; Appraisal Factors; What He Should Be; The Problem Areas; Style; Leaders are Made, Not Born; How It's Done; The Exit Interview; Discipline; Self-Policing Discipline; Communicating Discipline; Charisma; The Types of Leadership; The "New" Supervisor

10   The New Supervision   173
The Union-Free Work Group

Responsibilities of the Supervisor; People; Technical; Environment; The Company; Training in Communication; Upward Communication; Meetings and Writings; Rapport, Feedback; The Grapevine; Concern-Orientation; A Check-Up; Conclusion

11   The New Supervision   187
Ideas that Work

Written Aids; People Book; Work Record; Daily Plan; Calendar; Informal Notes; Technology; The Cassette Recorder; The Instant Camera; The Personal Bulletin Board; Employees' Bulletin Board; Task Forces; Oral Communication; Ombudsman; Rap Sessions; Listening; Patterned Conversation; Information; Suggestions; Opinion; Fruitful Questioning; Open-End Question; The Negative Question; Problem Question; Tail-End Question; Indirect Questioning; Question-and-Planted-Answer; The Summary Question; Come Off Courteous; Giving Orders; Appealing to Pride; Recognizing His Contribution; Personal Touch; Togetherness; Performance Review; Job Enrichment; Job Posting; Overtime Rotation; Contest; Work Simplification; Recruiting; Grievance Handling; Restating; Work Group Grievance Plan; Grievance Log; Conclusion

12   Labor Law & the Union-Free Supervisor   201

The Supervisor Defined; The Unfair Labor Practices; Board Election

Rules; Authorization Cards Honored; Pre-Drive Actions; The Undercover; Campaign; The Open Campaign; The Law's View; A General Rule

Conclusion   **212**

Index   **214**

Introduction

The *Union-Free Supervisor* is for the supervisor and managers, who are responsible for developing supervisors in plants, shops or offices that have union-free people.

It is the first book on supervising and personnel management that recognizes a difference between a place of work that is union-free and one that is unionized. It looks at the process by which a work group without a union becomes or refuses to become a group with a union.

There are vast differences in the job of the supervisor whose work group is union-free. These differences make it urgent that he learn all there is to learn about the organizing process and that he master his role in resisting the union's spread.

The first part of the *Union-Free Supervisor* contains a thorough analysis of the impact of unionism and the actual effects of having a union on the company, the worker and on the supervisor. How a union organizes employees and how a company must respond to stay union-free, both in the long run and short run, is examined. The special problems of the white collar group and the union-free group that is a "pocket" in a unionized workplace are examined. The first section ends with a look at the ideas and messages we can expect a union and a company to use.

The second part concerns the key man in the union-free picture, the employee, and the company's key man, the supervisor. The job of the supervisor and the things he should be doing to better himself are studied. Finally, the law of labor organizing is put into perspective for the union-free supervisor.

Each reader brings a unique background to this book and will be looking for the things that he needs from it. It is recommended, though, that every supervisor and manager read how the union organizes and the company defends. There are important cues for the leader in what he should be trying to do, and more important, *when* he should do it. Also, he should look at the samples of union and company messages that may be seen in a campaign. The variety is eye-opening.

Every supervisor should study the chapter on the law of union organizing. The key knowledge here is that the law does not muffle the company or the supervisor.

In preparing this manuscript, the author has assumed that:

The employer is subject to the jurisdiction of the National Labor Relations Board.

Both company and union will attempt to stay within the law. The great publicity given those cases in which a company or a union has gone afoul of the law obscures the reality that nearly all labor-management relations are carried out legally.

The union has chosen to organize by consent of the employees; not to organize "from the top" either by collusion or force.

Though there are references to the law of organizing, this is not a law book and it must not be looked upon as legal advice.

The supervisor must remember than many of these matters are closely involved with management policy. He must always be sure he is acting as one with his management before he acts on his own.

Finally, the effective supervisor will consider this volume only a beginning. There is much yet to be learned about supervising union-free people.

Union-Free Supervisor

Union & Company

Chapter 1

The Impact of Unionism

The pickup truck clanked to a halt at the silent water scrubber unit. Its driver, a member of the Truck Driver - Heavy Equipment Operator craft, climbed out stiffly, stretched and yawned. His passengers, a Rigger and his helper, turned their attention to the load, a pump that was to be installed in place of an ailing one that had caused the shutdown of the scrubber. The Riggers unlimbered an "A"-frame, handily tied on to the new pump and set it down gently near the equipment it would replace.

A Pipefitter and his helper were dropped off from another pickup while the pump was being lowered, but drifted away with the Riggers for a smoke when they found the job had not progressed to the point where their skills could be used. An electrician, and then an insulator, each trailed by a helper, arrived on the scene in a few minutes and began disconnecting the electrical connections and stripping off the insulating material from the pipes. The Pipefitters returned and broke the pipe connections. The Riggers went back into action, removing the inoperable pump by means of an overhead crane and placing the new one into alignment, under the guidance of the Pump Mechanics, who had been in touch with the entire procedure since they carried primary responsibility for changing out the pump.

After the pump was carefully leveled and in working order the show began to run backward, with the various crafts adding their touches until the pump was started up and the scrubber was back on stream. The Electricians had been some half hour late coming back on the job, having become involved in changing burned-out light bulbs in another part of the plant (a task they zealously guarded as their exclusive duty). The truck driver had been standing by through the full job to haul off tools, the old pump, and assorted craftsmen and helpers.

The entire job was within the ability of a good general mechanic and one helper and could have been performed in a fraction of the time this intricate interplay of narrow skills consumed.

Featherbedding in industry today is not confined to the notorious railroads, print shops and docks. This pump changeout occurred in a plant where the maintenance function was under the jurisdiction of a single union. The practices were imposed by the union; they were not a result of the competition for work that often breaks out among the craft unions.

Inefficient? The plant management felt it fortunate that the pump had not failed at night. In that event it would have been necessary to call in a tool room attendant in addition to all the craftsmen and all their helpers, paying each one the minimum, for the call-in, of four hours even though his portion of the job might require only a few minutes and he would be able to return home.

Union-Free Management Dartnell 1968

The Supervisor's Challenge

The supervisor in a union-free plant, office or shop would shake his head in disbelief at the complicated, cumbersome work rules in unionized workplaces. Such work practices make it hard for supervisors in unionized plants to meet their responsibilities for output and quality. The task of the supervisor in a union-free operation is quite different: more demanding, but certainly more rewarding.

The union-free supervisor will be called upon to help defend against a union's attempt to seize power among his workers. He may in fact be called upon before any union appears, to take action that will reduce the chances of a union success, which will itself reduce the likelihood that any union will appear. The open organizing attempts happen when the union's chances are best.

The union-free supervisor should gladly accept this responsibility. He may not feel strongly about unionism; he may, in fact, have a favorable opinion of unionism, perhaps through friendship with unionists and union officials. Most unionists are due respect and are quite sincere in what they are doing. A few supervisors will have had favorable experiences as members of unions or have heard of cases where unions have performed well for all concerned. But, all things considered, the union presence is clearly undesirable.

A union will promise workers freedom from exploitation by giving them higher pay, job protection, more fringe benefits, a system for the handling of complaints, an end to favoritism and a signed contract covering the employer-employee relation. The promises are attractive, though a union is often unable to deliver on its promises after it has become bargaining agent. The key point, though, is that having a union brings problems; much that is bad comes intó the picture along with any good it may bring.

In a typical firm with skilled, enlightened management, the effect of the union way of operation on the company, the employees and ultimately the supervisor himself, can only be damaging. It behooves the supervisor to put forth real effort to prepare himself to meet the union's challenge.

Effect on the Company

The impact of the union condition on a company is of three general types: a loss of freedom to act arising from national labor law, the inefficiencies inherent in the union-management relationship and the profit erosion that results from management's giving up its rights in labor contract negotiations.

National Labor Law

Government regulation of employer action is an ever-present fact when the union is trying to organize employees. The drain on profit due to these regulations is greater, though, when the company has been unionized:

1. The law has been interpreted to mean that management cannot make a business decision that will cause loss of jobs or affect the employees, unless it first negotiates with its union about the decision. The decision itself is the subject of this bargaining, not just the effect of the decision on jobs or other job-related problems. Employers have been ordered to re-open plants that had been shut down because they were losing money, since they had not bargained with the union about the decision. Management decisions to contract out work that had been performed less efficiently by members of the bargaining unit have been overturned, again because it had not bargained about the

decision to contract. Bargaining has also been required on decisions to automate, to sell a plant, to move a plant or office and to drop a product line.

2. Union restrictions of a worker's output have been enforced by law in decisions that permit the union to punish members who exceed work norms by fining them or barring them from membership. Unions are upheld in refusing to work with new products, as a housing contractor who attempted to use pre-fabricated doors discovered. The union instead demanded, and got, the right to build the doors.

3. The courts have held that the duty to bargain includes the obligation to arbitrate matters that may not be covered in the labor contract, the question of need to arbitrate being left to an arbitrator and not to a judge.

The Situation

An even greater drain on the company's resources and strength lies in the basics of the employer-union relationship. Here is a conflict of objectives that cannot be reconciled.

A union in a plant or office is somewhat on the defensive with its own membership. It must forever be proving that its value to them is at least equal to its cost in terms of dues, fees and assessments. In most locals there is a rival "splinter" group ready to step in if the incumbents make too many mistakes. Willingness to understand the management's viewpoint will be labeled a "sell-out" by this opposition within. Never-ending pressure and bickering between seniority groups, crafts, ethnic groups or work shifts leave the union leadership forever needing a victory. The inter-group tensions take a heavy toll on teamwork and productivity.

The union will use its bargaining power in those areas in which it can show tangible results: security from loss of jobs; rising wage scale and fringe benefits; security from economic loss through personal disability, old age or business conditions; and security from unjust or arbitrary action of supervisors.

However laudable these aims, the employer cannot embrace them all. An employer cannot grant absolute security. Most employers will provide as much security as practical, but that is never enough in the union view. The management must busy itself with the security of the business and with optimizing the return on the owners' investment. This, in the management view, is the best kind of security for the workers since it alone makes the other brands of security possible.

Also inherent in the union-management situation is the ill effect of the union's weapons of power on profit. Most obvious is the strike; but also the union-inspired grievances, the revolt against authority, the dissension and unfriendliness that too often mark the unionized group. In some cases there are deliberate attempts to damage the company.

The company had refused to recognize the union at a distant company location and otherwise, allegedly, treated non-union people more favorably. Union officers got time off from work to distribute literature to incoming workers, literature which turned out to be:

". . . This company is using their powers to influence members of our union to abandon the principles of unity. We all know, I am sure, what the ultimate aim is. Without a strong union, which we now have, a return to the so-called good old days would only be around the corner. Inclosed is a suggested letter that you may **send along with your mutilated credit card** to _____ Inc . . . "

The company, feeling that this pressure to let the union in at the other location with no election was improper, attempted to stop distribution of the leaflets. An NLRB trial examiner declared that stopping it was an unfair labor practice.

Most damaging of all, perhaps, are the philosophy and work practices that spring from certain long-held union goals for the worker.

The Seniority Principle

Strict adherence to seniority wherever possible in the job scene has become a trademark of the union presence. Of course, seniority is applicable and appropriate in many matters—length of vacation, choice of vacation periods, lay-offs (where qualifications are substantially equal), amount of pension, choice of jobs (again, where qualification is not an issue), and similar matters. But as the only method of selection for promotion it is almost ludicrous; it is a coincidence when the senior man is also the best man for the job.

The unions themselves rarely use seniority as a basis for choosing their key committee heads and their skilled staff men. The company loses its ability to challenge its most productive people by offering financial reward and promotion; the effect on the high-ability men who lose the promotion is devastating.

Unions have no stake in rewarding ability; they have, in the short run, nothing to lose from full use of seniority. They favor seniority because it is easy to measure and settling intramembership disputes on a simple seniority basis makes for easier politicking for the union in-group. It also makes for easier organizing, since it is likely at any given time in a union-free firm there will be fewer workers who have benefited from a merit system than those who have been by-passed by a less senior man. The employer always runs the risk of seeming to play favorites in its honest attempt to reward merit. Favoritism is a prime dissatisfier for an organizer to exploit.

Job Narrowing

On the issue that workers must not be "speeded up and stretched out," unions will usually press for greater specialization, a narrower range of individual duties, and sharply defined jobs. Restrictions of this type may have served a social purpose when sweatshop conditions were commonplace, but they are of small service today. The unions' goal in this is, on the surface, to make work easier for its members. As a practical matter, to staff a given operation more employees must be hired when duties are narrowed. This, in turn, means more dues payers for the union.

Reduction of Output

In an exercise of the same principle as in job narrowing, the unions will encourage the workers to perform at the minimum level of output that the employer will accept. By informal means workers are pressured to produce at lower levels, and not be "rate busters" in incentive systems. These pressures are not always "informal", since workers in recent years have gone to court in protest of union discipline imposed on them for exceeding union output norms. The courts have usually upheld the unions' discipline.

This is not just an idle argument with excellence on the part of the unions, nor is it just a carry-over from the construction industry (where it is clear there is a fixed amount of work to be done, and the sooner it is completed, the sooner unemployment begins if there is no other job in sight). It is also the need for additional workmen and the bigger "take" in dues, that a union can see in the slower hands and the dragging feet.

Equal Pay for Equal Work

The practice of paying a fixed rate for a particular set of duties is a motivation-killer without equal. The damage done by so ignoring varying ability, knowledge, skills, initiative, leadership, energy and work habits is hard to calculate.

A union has no use for excellence in production. On the contrary, a more mechanical pay system makes for easy administration, eliminates a source of jealousy between members and simplifies bargaining.

Relinquishment of Management Rights

The worst effect of unionization on profit is the employer giving up his rights in labor contract negotiations with the union. A union surely has a legitimate concern with the pay and benefits its members receive for the work that the company chooses to have them perform. But the unions' great contribution to inefficiency has come about through their bargaining about *what the job shall be.*

simply not agreeing to any wasteful practice. But the proposals come one by one in negotiations; the isolated concession seems cheap by comparison with the cost of not securing an agreement and taking a strike. A proposal that later proves costly may have seemed harmless and not worth opposing at the time it was negotiated. Also, inefficiencies may be conceded in day-to-day operations by not enforcing the labor agreement strictly, by loose contract interpretation or through arbitration. Even a partial list of these rights that employers have, at times, surrendered is staggering. The work practices that result are unheard of in the union-free plant or office and mostly unwanted by the workers. The following are rights a company often surrenders in labor negotiations.

Right to contract work out, both in service areas—guards, custodial employees, etc.—and in the regular work of the employer, even when that work can be performed more economically by a contractor.

Right to shut down part or all of the operation or to move the plant or office.

Right to require overtime work and to use on this work the men most needed. This is often relinquished by the establishment of an overtime rotation system (which will typically give the worker the right to decline to work).

Right to regulate leaves for personal reasons.

Right to determine the size and mix of the work force.

Right to assign work to another unit of the company (but outside the bargaining unit).

Right to preserve seniority for foremen and supervisors, both for those promoted out of the bargaining unit and those who had been promoted from the ranks before the union came in.

Right to create new production methods, or to install new facilities where it might affect jobs in the bargaining unit.

One of the key issues in the protracted 1969 longshoremen strike was the union's demand to unpack and re-pack containers in mid-shipment. These containers had been designed to be part of a system where final packing can be done at the point of production and the container shipped via surface, sea, then surface again to point of use. The employers surrendered to the union's "make-work" proposal.

Right to spread the work to avoid laying off junior people by reducing hours, or even by reducing overtime.

Right to move employees laterally to a shift or a job for qualification rather than seniority.

Right to fix standards of performance, to set the quality or quantity of output, rather than to accept union-imposed production limitations, make-work practices and featherbedding.

Right to establish work rules and to discharge employees for those offenses which may fall short of criminal or for criminal-type offenses for which no court action is to be taken.

Right to forbid union activity on company time (larger plants often will have stewards on the payroll with no other duties than their union dealings).

Right to determine the content and duties of the job and to change the work load of an employee.

Right to select new employees and to make initial assignments for seasoning.

Right to establish and enforce safety rules.

Right to use labor-saving equipment and methods.

Right to set prices.

Right to lay off, re-assign, to schedule overtime work, etc., without notice if necessary.

Right to retire employees.

Right to observe an adequate probationary period for a new employee.

Right to consider, as a basis for promotion, employees' attitudes, habits, punctuality, attention, absenteeism, education, workmanship, energy level, teamwork, cooperation with supervision or fellow workers, and potential for later growth.

Right to leave temporary vacancies unfilled when unneeded—and to fill them when needed with the best available employee.

Right to use tests for new employee selection, for selecting employees for promotions, transfers and training opportunities.

Right to require training for promotion.

Right to select the best qualified employees for training.

Right to control the periods that vacations may be taken.

Right to transfer to avoid layoffs.

Right to assign technical or engineering personnel to perform experimental work within the unionized work area.

Right to discipline for poor quality work.

Right to grant individual merit pay increases or to have merit factor in progression increases.

Right to create new or change old, qualifications for jobs and to determine the level of skill of employees to be assigned to a job.

Right to establish new wage rates for new jobs.

Right to establish shift schedules.

Right to eliminate a classification.

Right of trainee, staff man or engineer to perform work of the bargaining unit. Right of the supervisor to use 20% of his time in work of the bargaining unit (as he may do without losing his exemption from provisions of the Fair Labor Standards Act).

Freedom to meet Equal Employment Opportunity obligations.

Right to depart from past practice.

Right to prevent union representatives (though they may be employees of competitors) from entering the plant and observing "trade secrets."

It is interesting to note that in this long detailing of some of the ill effects of unions on an employer, the matter of pay and benefits is not mentioned. A unionized employer can anticipate no great loss in this area, relative to employers who do not have unions. His loss is in his ability, and his right, to manage his work force and his investment.

Effect on Employees

The union will ground its claim to the loyalty of the workers on a promise of improvement in their lot. But how valid is this claim? Observing unionized work situations alongside union-free ones in today's intelligently managed operations, one is forced to the conclusion that the union-free worker has a much more satisfying work experience.

Where the plants are similar except that one has a union and the other does not, the union-free people seem to have more fulfilling work. They are happier, more involved with their work, and more productive. Though this is an undocumented observation it is a "feel" that is confirmed by the observations of great numbers of managers and industrial relations practitioners.

A union will usually promise more of the material things of pay and benefits, but here again is frustration for the workers because it becomes obvious that these factors are about the same in similar union and non-union shops, plants and offices. The unionized workers look about them and see comparable wages and fringes offered in union-free firms.

The presence of a political organization endowed with exclusive bargaining power causes bad feelings, cliques and friction among those seeking power. The leadership often finds it necessary to justify its own existence by stirring up dissatisfaction with the company.

But, consider these concrete reasons why the overall effect of unionism on employees is unfavorable:

Union-centered employee relations subordinates the individual to the group, giving up personal freedom to group power. Individual dignity is thrust to the rear and is given scant consideration.

The union goal of narrower job duties and greater specialization *runs counter to current opinion on what the worker really wants from his job.* The evidence today is that he wants a richer job, which in practice means that he should perform a wider range of tasks and be given *more* responsibility for his own performance.

Employers find themselves handling discipline mechanically, due to the threat of later review by an arbitrator. The weight of arbitrators' opinions in discipline cases teaches us that rules must be enforced strictly and discipline must be dealt out by rote in the union environment. Otherwise the rules won't stand up and the discipline will not hold if brought to arbitration. As one supervisor put it, "No matter how much you may want to let off with a warning the long-time employee who is caught removing supplies for his own use, you are forced to discharge him or face the prospect of being charged with discrimination before an arbitrator when you discharge a new worker for an offense." Similarly, a worker found guilty of falsifying his original application for employment must be punished regardless of his years of good service, if the rule is to stand up for new employees. Extended leaves of absence without pay must be denied unless the labor agreement clearly permits it.

No matter how good its intentions, the company gradually finds itself unable to make "personalized" decisions about its people, when they are represented by a labor union.

Similarly, employees lose their personal relationship with the company's management when a union is in the picture. A man can no longer go to his boss with work problems, but must clear them through his union representative. Pay increases are handled on an across-the-board basis rather than on a basis of merit. The union is quite satisfied with mediocrity in the work force. The above-mediocre workman is frustrated.

The foremen in a unionized plant may regard the individual as no more than a member of a crowd. His ability to get along with the union stewards is affected by the extent to which he adopts their standards in dealing with the membership. The union's way of human relations is that way which is most mechanical.

The most subtle indictment of unionization is not just the union's treating the individual human as a predictable and unimportant unit, but the employer's doing precisely the same thing, due to a variety of direct and indirect pressures from the union.

The mere presence of a union causes controversy because some employees are for it and some are against it. This is true not only of the organizing period, there is rivalry between these factions, so long as an anti-union group exists. It is stacked on the troubles caused by rivals seeking power within the union. It leads to disputes, ill feeling between cliques, broken friendships and disharmony throughout the work life.

Employees in a union are subject to fines for violation of union rules, reporting violations of plant rules, producing beyond amounts approved by the union and crossing any picket lines.

In a 1971 NLRB case Union A and Union B had separate contracts covering the units they represented within the same plant. Union A went on strike when negotiating for a new contract.

Union B had a no-strike clause in its contract (which was not then open for negotiation). However, the members of Union B were informed by their shop steward that they were to observe Union A's picket line and not report for work. Seven members of B did not obey him, but respected their no-strike clause and reported to work during A's strike.

One of the seven was fined $275 and the other six were fined $1,000 by the union!

The NLRB held that the fines were lawful and that the amount of the fines did not affect their lawfulness. Fines of this kind can usually be collected through court action, like a debt.

Employees are exposed to strikes which can produce violence, property damage, hatred, loss of pay and even loss of the job.

Employees must pay costly dues which may not be wisely spent by the union leadership; they are pressured to contribute to political candidates and lobbying activities that they may personally oppose and to dubious financial practices with welfare funds, in some unions.

There is no easy way out of the unionized condition. For the employees, it is virtually a one-way street. Once a union has become the bargaining agent and has gained the power that goes along with that status, it can bring countless pressures on the people in its bargaining unit to remain members. Under union-shop contracts, in states that permit them, the individual has to stay in the union to keep his job. The NLRB has ruled in favor of a union which expelled members for supporting a petition to the Board for a decertification election, in an attempt to free themselves from the union.

Effect on the Nation

Our nation cannot escape the ill effects of the enrollment of a substantial percentage of the work force in labor unions. These effects are due, in large part, to restrictions that are placed on an employee's ability and creativity. Featherbedding, forcing the employer to accept work and workers that he doesn't want or need, has been estimated to have cost the railroads alone $500,000,000 a year for work not done.

The unions' long-standing insistence that railroads employ a fireman to serve on a diesel engine (to shovel coal to an internal combustion engine?) is only one of thousands of situations where railroads pay for work not performed or for work performed that is not needed. Others are "Interchange" rules under which crews of different railroads lay claim to switching privileges at a single site. A crew may take a load of another line's cars to the other yard, but cannot bring back its own cars on the return trip; rules requiring assignment of engineers, conductors or brakemen to equipment actually operated by "maintenance of way" employees, resulting in a rail detector car having an engineer and three trainmen along for the ride (some railroads will pay such extra people to stay home, to keep from overcrowding a section crew's motor car); and "Hostling" agreements that give road crews extra pay just to bring their engine to the train.

Some of the more ruinous of these "make-work" practices may be melting slowly in the heat of recent arbitration board awards and contract settlements.

No estimate is available of the cost of featherbedding in, for instance, the printing industry or the construction industry but the bill must be staggering.

Strikes have a profound effect on the nation's wealth. The goods and services lost due to strikes are lost forever to the national standard of living (this is true also of wasteful work practices). The standard of living can be no more or less than the goods and services that are available to the consumers.

Inflation is encouraged by union action. No one can seriously maintain that unions are alone responsible for inflation, but they can cause the restrictions of output and, in those industries where they have high leverage, the abnormal wage increases that assuredly contribute to inflation.

A specific effect on the nation of the union presence was demonstrated by Victor Riesel in his calculations which showed that actions of organized labor had cost the space program enough time to allow the USSR to be first into outer space. Job action of the unions included strikes, slowdowns, and forced duplication of work.

The excesses at Cape Canaveral included such activities as demanding that cables already manufactured be destroyed and reproduced by the union people at the Cape; that extensive tests already made be rerun at the Cape and that wiring work which could be done far more efficiently elsewhere, be done at the Cape. Strikes and threats of strikes enforced these demands.

Fair Employment Threatened

Equal employment opportunity has been adopted as national policy by legislation and by executive order; certain unions have been scored repeatedly for their failure to cooperate in achieving it. With special reference to the building trades, the Equal Employment Opportunities Commission has charged that certain craft unions discriminate. They control access to employment through their rigid control of the hiring process and when they refuse to admit minorities to membership they simply deny them opportunities for construction employment. The condition cannot be corrected by a great splurge of admissions of minority members since the craft unions deliberately limit the numbers of craftsmen leaving few vacancies.

A 1969 nationwide survey showed that black membership in five major craft unions totaled only 1,421 of a total membership of nearly 330,000. The Plumbers and Sheetmetal Workers had 0.2% blacks; the Electrical Workers 0.6%, the Elevator Constructors 0.4% and the Asbestos Workers 0.9%. Only the Laborers, lowest paid of the building trades, had a large percentage (30.5) of Blacks.

How damaging to the national interest is our growing inability to compete with foreign manufacturers in the overseas market and, more recently, in the domestic marketplace? The spiraling cost of United States labor (relative to the competition) is believed the major cause of this state of affairs. Labor costs, of course, are a mixture of climbing wage rates, the inefficient work practices, the strike (made more menacing by the threat of coalition bargaining, now being demanded by certain industrial unions) and the union attitude toward the work. The problem of "runaway" ships from the U.S. Merchant Marine (U.S. - owned vessels registered in other nations) is usually laid to the U.S. unions' high and ever-growing wage rates, their make-work practices and resistance to work-saving innovation. The products in international trade in which we are still competitive tend to be those that are new developments or those in which the production tools and method are the chief factor of cost. Both of these can be attributed largely to our researchers and technologists, who are largely union-free people.

A final indictment of the union way of running the workplace is its effect on worker attitudes. In a free system which has grown great by its emphasis on the power and dignity of the individual human personality, the union presence reduces him to a grumbling working stiff. The union principles that seniority must rule, that work must be simplified, that output must be held to the minimum possible and that it should all pay the same are certain to have an effect on the humans that are touched. Applied systematically to millions of single events, their effect on the national personality is sure to surface in time.

Much of this resembles "What's good for General Motors is good for America" reasoning. But, again, it is clear that the total quantity of goods and services produced truly makes up the nation's standard of living. Anything serving to reduce that production reduces that standard. More importantly, any force that erodes a person's individuality, self-sufficiency, dignity and desire to grow damages the real wealth of our nation.

Effect on Supervisors

The one person most deeply affected by the presence of a union is the supervisor. His job is changed more than any other by the advent of a union. Less demanding in some respects, his work becomes far more frustrating as fewer of the real sources of job satisfaction are left to him.

The textbooks concede no differences between a unionized and union-free shop or plant. The "how-to" books for supervisors suggest no difference in his behavior in the two situations. But there are vast differences. The employer with no union can delegate the great bulk of the "people decisions" about employees to the first-line supervisor. Such employer actions as promotion, training, transfer, merit pay increases, change of job duties, assignment and withdrawal of responsibilities, temporary upgrading, assignment to key jobs, granting leaves of absence, discharge and suspension all can be within the authority of the supervisor, the man responsible for getting out the work. Surely this is a better state of affairs for the company. It can be better for the employee, depending on the supervisor. But who can argue that it is not *different?*

If the employee is a loser when a union comes in and the company is a loser, the foreman is the greatest loser of all. Examine certain of the disadvantages to employees: strikes, bad feelings, cliques, friction, dissatisfaction with the company, grievances, powerless employees, inefficient work practices, poor discipline, misconduct, and frustration. The foreman stands between the battle lines of employee-employee conflict and employee-company dissatisfaction. The foreman is usually the focus of employee feelings in a strike and perhaps the object of violence.

The foreman's control of job duties and the power to construct jobs, even where the effects are most beneficial to the employees, is gone. The union is sensitive to the slightest change of job duties, fearful that "generalization" will creep in. The supervisor's power to transfer (there are countless cases where an employee is better fitted for work in another department or perhaps is not performing up to par where he is and stands a good chance to succeed somewhere else) goes by the boards when a union installs a bidding and seniority system on open jobs, even on lateral transfers. To have anything resembling the man he wants on the job, the supervisor in the union system must approach it negatively, disqualifying those obviously not qualified.

The supervisor's stature in complaint settlement crumbles. Where his decision often is final in a union-free plant, he is only the lightly-regarded first step in the typical labor contract grievance procedure. He is responsible for training but a) use of a training program may be regulated by the union contract, b) a seniority system may remove his ability to select candidates and c) even the content of a training course has been challenged. An oil company held meetings (with pay) to explain the case for the depletion allowance and its importance to the success of the company, but the union filed a complaint with the NLRB charging that this amounted to changing working conditions without bargaining.

The book, *How to Be a More Effective Union Representative,** has a chapter entitled "How to Build a Fire under the Foreman." When a department is "... stuck with a foreman who," as the author puts it, "can't get along with his men or the union, the union must either persuade the foreman to mend his ways or get rid of him." The method, it says, is quite simple: the union representative and the men agree to snow the foreman under with grievances, with the foreman as the cause of the complaints. The steward pushes the grievances up to the third stage where the representative and top management handle the grievances.

The representative hammers away constantly at the foreman, saying he can't get along, can't get out the production. The company will know that most of the grievances are phony, but becomes concerned at the wrangling between the foreman and his men (the other departments have been advised not to file any grievances, for the time, that embarrass their foremen).

The book says the company will support the foreman at first but at length, perhaps after months, the pressure becomes too great and the management will advise the foreman, privately, to make peace or face being transferred. The company will not admit the true reason for the transfer, but it will happen, at a time when things are relatively quiet.

"One of the fringe benefits of this technique is that it sets an example for all the other foremen ... they know the same thing can happen to them ... it is possible to get almost any foreman to cooperate with the union—or get rid of him—by snowing him under."

The supervisor still carries the responsibility for getting the work out, but without the same authority over his men. The authority itself is missed; the subtle need to direct others, to render discipline. The even more subtle need to "do" for others is frustrated.

He has been the embodiment of the company to the workers and the point of contact for most communication, up or down the organization. He has been the ultimate yes or no on many matters and his word was respected in all "people decisions." The great loss to the supervisor is being stripped of power and purpose by the workings of the unionized organization.

Conclusion

This has not been an attempt to balance the pros and cons of unionism. It is simply a listing of the most obvious cons. It is intended

---

* Duane Beeler and Harry Kurshenbaum. *How to Be a More Effective Union Representative.* Chicago: Roosevelt University Press, 1965.

to show that there are many good reasons for a supervisor, a manager, employee or an interested citizen to oppose the spread of unions.

Most supervisors strongly believe that a union on the work scene is not good for the company, the supervisor or the working man or woman. A few would agree that it is not good for the company or themselves, but (based perhaps on their own experience elsewhere) it *is* good for the workers and thus worthwhile, at least in some companies.

Those who believe this must face two questions: Does a man who works for *me* need a union to be treated fairly? Does a man who works for *my* company need a union to be treated fairly?

The supervisor will be expected to assume the main burden of the person-to-person communication that is needed to discourage the approach of unions and to defend against the union that does approach. This burden he should accept with real enthusiasm and dedication because it is his company, his people and himself who will benefit if he is successful.

Chapter 2
How & Why a Union Organizes

"Joe, did you see those guys out on the parking lot this morning, passing out handbills for a union?"

"Yeah," Joe replied to his fellow foreman as they entered the snack bar, "I saw them, but I haven't seen the handbills. What did they say?"

"Funny. It was a sort of general thing about human dignity and the rights of man, and it said everybody ought to join a union, but it didn't even mention the company, only the name of some union local and its telephone number."

"They'll never get anywhere that way. Our people are not going to buy anything if it doesn't get in there and call a spade a spade. They haven't got a chance!"

This incident tells us that the chances are excellent that the company will be unionized within a short time. The supervisors are naive concerning union organizing methods and hopelessly uninformed about the particular union that is organizing their men. They appear to know nothing about its activity among the men and in the community in the recent past.

How the Union Campaigns

The union bid for the power to act for the workers is not an impulsive, haphazard affair. It is usually a planned, business-like, goal-oriented program. Its goal is to cause the employer to recognize the union as exclusive agent for the employees. The union may seek this recognition direct from the employer (by persuasion, threat or picketing), or through a "card check" or an informal election by agreement with the employer. But ordinarily the union will seek it through an NLRB election. If in this election over half of the voting employees select a union, the employer is required by law to recognize that union and bargain with it; the employer can no longer deal directly with the individual employee. It is this method of gaining recognition that we will study in detail here.

The union's campaign for the vote of the men will be conducted, in most cases, by a full-time employee of the union. This man will likely have other duties involving negotiation and contract administration for groups already organized. He may receive help from other professional full-time union staff men or from organizers on a temporary or part-time basis (usually union workers taking time off from their jobs for short-term union employment). The typical union contract will have a provision that a worker may take leave of absence without pay, for service with the union without loss of company seniority. Free help is sometimes available from other organized groups of the same union in the area and from strong union supporters among the workers of the company being organized.

The organizer himself may have been recruited from college by the union in competition with corporate recruiters, he may have come from the ranks of the workers, as a member who has shown exceptional talent in union affairs, or he may have gained his experience in previous employment with other unions. Whatever his background, he will have been trained in the techniques of organizing both in the formal classroom setting and on-the-job, under the guidance of experienced organizers. He will typically be a likeable guy. He will have natural human relations and leadership ability; he will be able to meet people easily, to communicate well and to understand employee problems.

The Four Phases of Campaigning

In studying the campaign itself it is helpful to consider each type of campaign activity separately. In most campaigns there is an exploratory phase, a sub rosa (underground) phase, then an open phase. The last, the open electioneering, is best examined in two parts: that period before an election is scheduled and an immediate pre-election phase. So there are four phases to be studied, with four different kinds of activity and employer counter-activity going on. Here we shall be looking at the activity in terms of the union's action. The countermeasures will be covered in detail later.

There is nothing official about these phases. They exist only in the abstract, to describe the sort of actions that may take place. There is overlapping and often no clear marker denoting the end of one phase and the start of another. There often may be a lapse of time between exploratory and active campaigning action. There may even be lapses of days, even months, within a phase (though rarely in the final campaign). Lapses are usually due to the organizer's absence.

The Exploratory Phase

CLERKS - TYPISTS - SECRETARIES . . . Are you unhappy with your present job? Inquire about higher pay and improved working conditions. Call 221-7311 or write in confidence to Classified Ad Box No. 392.

The dissatisfied steno calling that number in the Help Wanted columns may be surprised to find, after she has revealed the name of her employer, that she is in touch with a union, rather than a company seeking her services. This union is zeroing in on employee groups that are prospects for organizing.

One of the nation's largest unions stages exhaustive surveys, covering entire metropolitan areas, of all the jobs within its jurisdiction in non-union stores, shops, and plants. It will gather information on pay, benefits, working hours, work practices, and location of workers' homes. Again, zeroing in on prospective bargaining units.

Union organizers study the business sections of newspapers for news of new plants that are planned and, interestingly, for news of layoffs or financial difficulties of non-union employers in their area. Nothing is so shattering to employee morale as the layoff of fellow workers. Financial trouble for an employer will cause deep feelings of insecurity among its workers.

The "Help Wanted" ad, the regional labor market survey and the rapt interest in business news are examples of general exploratory moves designed to pinpoint the most attractive targets for concentrated organizing efforts.

When a target employer is picked, the union's first steps are also exploratory. The organizer will consult the information available to his own union and to other unions in the area about the employer's labor relations history. Have there been organizing drives in the past and how did the company react? Has the company had strikes in the past? Is it a "paternalistic" employer, sponsoring athletic teams, picnics, employee social functions, credit unions, company clubs? Are there workers in the shop or office who have been active in a union before?

Company Information needed. From sources which may include the local Chamber of Commerce or manufacturers association the organizer (perhaps posing as a sales executive) will compile information such as :

Ownership and financing of the company. Is ownership local or absentee?

Location of other units of the company. Is this location underpaid relative to other company units? Are they unionized?

Profit picture of the company and of the particular plant or shop under study, if it is a multi-location company. Not that a decision to organize or not to organize will be based on the finding. The purpose is mainly to impress upon the workers that an outside organizer has the facts on matters such as these, possibly better than they themselves have.

The company's role locally: a corporate "good citizen?"

The identity of dominant or well-known executives.

The status of any construction work the company has under way locally.

From other sources, perhaps former employees, a nearby bartender or barber or simply close observation:

The means by which the firm ships and receives; this bears on the company's ability to keep operating during a strike.

The age and condition of the plant, shop, or office. Physical working conditions may be an important dissatisfier.

Location of the gates or entrances. The union's ability to communicate with the employees is affected by the extent to which they mass to enter and leave.

Number of floors or physically separated departments.

Starting and quitting times, shift change times.

Transportation facilities used by the workers.

Approximate number of employees in each department.

Composition of the work force in respect of sex, age, race and nationality.

The last item, bearing on the social organization within the target group, is of prime importance to the organizer. Is there a high percentage of females? Do they work in close proximity to the males? This information is needed to discover points of friction, to plan the content of communications. If the group is mixed, white and black, or by nationality, is there a good relationship between the groups? Jealousies in these areas are easy to play upon. Communications and leadership-recruiting must be planned with the predominating groups in mind. Is there a large group of rural people in the work force? These are considered hard nuts for an organizer to crack. Do the workers show high morale? Are the supervisors well-prepared and are they considered fair and impartial?

Variety of Approaches. Employers cannot afford to be lulled by the belief that the unions will follow any predictable pattern in exploring for likely targets. They are limited only by their imagination and their financial resources. The now-defunct UAW-Teamsters' Alliance for Labor Action employed advanced marketing techniques in a large-scale probe for prospects in the Atlanta area in 1969. Professionally developed materials which pictured the unions as devoted to community uplift were distributed in industrialized areas or industrial parks. No anti-employer messages and no authorization cards were to be found, only a return coupon to indicate interest and a telephone number to contact ALA headquarters if more information were needed. This was supported by full-page newspaper ads, also bearing a coupon for completion by those interested in " . . . bringing good wages and working conditions to unorganized workers . . ." Needless to say, replies were analyzed and follow-ups made with each one to isolate the most attractive targets for an orthodox full-scale campaign.

At any time in this underground phase the organizing activities can be halted, without great loss of money or time and with no loss of face. This decision may be the organizer's to make or it may be the international union's, acting on the organizer's findings, but either will know that this is the important decision—that much is to be lost if the campaign continues in spite of warning signs and then is unsuccessful. The decision may be a compromise to go on to the next step and set an early date for a final decision, which will take into account the union's progress to that date. In any event, all the information is carefully weighed and if results are clearly negative the campaign will be aborted and the organizer will go on to greener pastures.

The Sub Rosa Campaign

If the signs are good and the wind is right the organizer will move on into the second, sub rosa, stage of campaigning. The organizer is active, but tries to conceal his presence from the employer.

Again, these stages or phases have been isolated only for the purpose of studying a typical union organizing campaign. A particular "phase", as defined here, may not occur at all. There will nearly always be some kind of exploratory activity, but where the union has done it before in an unsuccessful attempt very little will be necessary (and many organizers think the best chance for success is on the second try). The sub rosa stage is sometimes skipped and open campaigning begins immediately. More often these days the sub rosa campaign is depended on to give the organizer all the support he will need and he can avoid expensive open campaigning.

This is the first point at which employees are contacted, and the organizer has three important objectives:

1. To find and develop employee leadership for the organizing to come.
2. To find issues—the grievances of the employees and other problems in the employee relationship.
3. To secure, if possible, authorization cards from as many as half the working force. Union authorization cards signed by a majority of the bargaining unit, even though they might have been signed under personal pressures, or just to keep the organizer from pestering, can lead to the company's being ordered by the NLRB to bargain with the union even though the election be lost or not held at all.

Developing Leadership. To find local leadership, the organizer will usually begin with a list of the names of a few employees who may be inclined toward unionism. They will have been found in the exploratory activity of the campaign. From these, and from "cold" contacts he may be making in the restaurant across the street or the bar where a few of the men stop for a drink after work, he will be learning who the unofficial leaders among the workers are. This leader is the man who has the confidence of his fellow workers. Consciously or not, he is the leader of his immediate group, building, floor or department in all important ways except in directing work.

Work direction is the supervisor's job and even in those cases where a supervisor is also the natural leader of the group there will always be a group member who is his counterpart in matters that do not involve the work. The organizer will attempt to contact each leader that he can identify and solicit his help in the organizing. Failing to get his active help, he will attempt to neutralize him; to get his agreement that he will neither oppose nor support the union. The organizer will then settle for the best leadership he can find among the others of that group.

A Leader Found. One organizer, analyzing the progess of the drive he was heading, found that it was a clear success in each of the four floors of the office except one; and on that floor there was not a single signed authorization card! The next day he discovered that the key was one Barney, a great natural leader who worked on that floor. Barney had not signed a card and though he was not outspoken against the union, none of the employees about him was inclined to sign a card until Barney did.

The organizer was equal to the occasion. He held a meeting at which the door prize was a color TV, first making sure that a friend of Barney's, who was also a friend of the union, would get Barney to attend. Would you believe Barney won the TV? And in the drawn-out process of delivering and installing the set the organizer finally asked Barney point-blank what he wanted of the union, in return for joining the union team. He answered quite readily that he wanted to be steward for his floor and a member of the Workmen's Committee. Easily done, Barney's floor came in 100%.

The organizer will try to enlist a leader for each recognizable, separate group within the work force. This may be a section, department or craft group or a locational, racial, political, national-origin or sex grouping. These people that he enlists become the campaign committee and they will usually become the leadership of the local union if the drive is successful.

The wise organizer will constantly evaluate the results of his work. Finding, soon after he begins seeking leadership, that the issues are not going to be persuasive and his recruitment is going badly, he will often content himself with establishing a "cell" and moving on.

The cell is composed of a handful of followers who have been well indoctrinated in union programs and policies. The organizer has done the indoctrinating in closed meetings, and has held out the promise of leadership in the future local union. Limited financial support is sometimes made available. The cell will quietly set about to enlarge its own ranks. Use of the "cell" is not confined to situations where the first attempt has failed—it is often the one method used, especially where stern opposition can be expected from the company or community.

The existence of a cell may be suspected after an open campaign has failed and perhaps its membership will be known. In an unsuccessful sub rosa drive, the drive itself may not have been discovered, so the cell almost surely can operate undetected.

Finding Issues. Identifying issues comes second in point of time. In the many contacts the organizer must make to form his organizing team, he will also be pointedly inquiring about the things that are frustrating the employees and causing dissatisfaction. He may set up a committee of new recruits to define the issues. He will discover if the company is violating any health, safety or wage law.

The organizer will always ask about the attitude of the foremen and supervisors. He will compile a record of their actions in the past that have seemed arbitrary or unfair to the workers and he will get the names of supervisors who have a reputation for being overbearing, unfair or self-important. He looks for these flaws because he knows that "personalizing" an issue gets him the most mileage. It is this kind of information that cannot be easily answered or refuted by the company. Other points he will cover:

Inequities in classification and wage rates within the company (he already knows the general wage level as compared to others in the area).

The method of awarding promotions or choice jobs (if it is not on a pure seniority basis, or another understandable systematic basis, he will know that there are some who consider themselves wronged).

Method of assigning overtime (again, if it is not being done in a mechanical way, he will know someone's feelings have been hurt).

Safety conditions of the building and equipment and safety awareness of the management (there is no more explosive issue than unsafe conditions).

Physical comfort of the workplace, be it plant, shop, or office—toilets, lighting, heating, seats, noise, crowding.

Adequacy of health and pension programs, their cost, and the fairness and speed of their administration.

These are the classic "dissatisfiers" and these are the things that are important to the organizer, though in a negative way. A company's bare adequacy or excellence in these are the same to him, and of no use. But inadequacy in any of them can present him with a major issue.

Gathering Cards. Bringing in the signed cards is the third objective of the sub rosa campaign, though a lesser one than the key goals of recruiting leaders and finding complaints and problems. As he works at finding leaders and issues, the organizer will be soliciting signed forms that authorize the union to act as the individual's bargaining agent. He will secure a card from each of his new leaders and from others he has contacted but whom he did not consider leadership material.

The soliciting of cards may become a sub-phase of the sub rosa period, with the newly found leaders assisting in a quiet card-pushing campaign. In a small shop or office the campaign may elect to make sub rosa card gathering the major effort, never surfacing with open campaigning unless the majority is found. The main campaign may also be kept under cover in a locale where unionism is strongly opposed by community leaders.

In contrast to a few years ago, the card-gathering activity has gained great importance. This occurred as the NLRB in the mid-60's turned out decisions ordering companies to bargain, based on the union's possession of signed cards from a majority of the bargaining unit. When he can count such a majority, the organizer may choose to demand immediate recognition of the company and if the company clearly knows the union has a majority, but will not accept the union, the NLRB has ruled it a refusal to bargain. Again, if the employer engages in serious unfair labor practices (theoretically rendering an election futile) the NLRB has ordered bargaining even though the union has lost the election. In this situation the union must have had the card majority, but need not have displayed it to the employer. Finally, if the employer a) has been offered card proof of a majority, but, b) has declined to recognize the validity of the cards, then, c) engages in unfair labor practices of the not-so-serious sort, the NLRB can be expected to order bargaining.

The organizer may still abort the campaign at any time in the sub rosa stage if things are not going well, without serious loss of face. If this is the decision, he will usually call together those he has recruited and break the news. This will be an emotion-packed meeting and he will ask them to continue to work quietly, promising the union will be back when the time is ripe. He will perhaps organize a formal "cell" which will continue to work under his very distant supervision.

The effort has not been completely wasted. The union will take with it a valuable list of "inside" men for use, as the organizer promised, if the situation later looks more favorable. If the union judges it has no future there, the list may be used for trade with another union which has designs on the group.

If the campaign is going well the organizer will be having home meetings of his leaders and committees to train them for the campaign ahead, and to get them involved with the success of the union.

The Open Campaign—No Election Pending

Another "all systems go" decision and the organizer is ready for the open campaign. He has not requested recognition; an election is not scheduled. Again, this stage may not occur at all if the organizer feels his sub rosa campaign has gained the support he needs to win an election or to persuade the employer that the union is in his future.

There is no standard move at this point. The organizer's judgment may be to go ahead with a relatively low-pressure card-signing campaign, or perhaps card-signing supported by a leaflet campaign. The fireworks will come later. In either case the cards will be "pushed" mainly by the employee supporters and mainly inside the plant or office. The leaflets at this point may be very general in nature, perhaps a "canned" handout printed by the International, since its only purposes are to show the union's face in support of the card-signing and to allow the organizer to introduce himself to a wider group while handing out the flyers. An Industrial Union Department handbook for organizers says, "As long as the leaflet names the union and includes something about the philosophy of the labor movement . . . it will serve its purpose . . . "

The moment the organizer allows employees to openly commit themselves is a key point. To this time he is free to come and go, to apply and release pressure. Many an employer has been puzzled by the early changes of pace in a campaign, believing the union has given up, only to see it return stronger than ever. He wonders if there is a mysterious grand strategy dictating these moves. Most often it is simply that the organizer had more pressing business elsewhere.

It is perhaps misleading to speak of "the organizer." It is done here for simplicity. While one organizer will be in charge of a particular campaign, there will be two or more full-time staff men assigned to a campaign of good size or to several campaigns in a small area. The "lone wolf" is the exception.

A sophisticated ploy, by these organizers just before initiating an open campaign, is to make home calls on the foremen, rather than the workers they intend to recruit. Overtly, they will be seeking the tacit approval, even the active support of the supervisor group. They may point out that the union will get them higher pay, indirectly, by raising the pay levels of the people they supervise. They may promise them seniority status in the contract that will be negotiated. Actually the true purpose is diagnostic: discovering the state of supervisory morale, how well-informed they are and what can be expected in the matter of company resistance to organizing.

The union's goal in this stage is to get the number of card-signers that are needed to go to an election with a reasonable chance of success, 60 to 70% according to most sources. The minimum is 30%, which the NLRB requires to prove a "show of interest" that will justify holding an election. The organizer will not neglect to consolidate the support he already has.

Campaign Tactics. The open campaign, when it warms up, is marked by mass communication: handbilling, posters, meetings, telephone chains, and in larger employee groups a campaign newspaper, sound trucks, paid advertising on TV, radio and newspapers, barbecues, picnics, press conferences, sky writing—the sky's the limit. Union communication and the differing emphasis for different types of workers—plant, office, technical, professional—are discussed in Chapter 6.

A form of communication that brought a slap on the wrist from an NLRB trial examiner was an "invasion" technique adopted by a department store employee union. To organize non-union direct mail advertisers, unionists in great numbers invaded the union-free shops during working hours in groups of ten to twenty. Production was stopped as they solicited workers at their work stations over the protests of the supervisors.

The solicitors were union members taking time off from their regular jobs in the vicinity, under the supervision of the union's staff organizers. Each organizer had been assigned the unorganized shops within a specified target area and the worker-organizers had been ordered from their work stations. A trial examiner found the method coercive and forbade the union's further use of it.

Committee activity aimed at involving more and more employees is stepped up now. There may be committees on strategy, issues, distribution, social activity, telephone, perhaps even a negotiating committee, though it's a little early for that.

The Demand for Recognition. Usually at a point in the open campaign (if there has been an open campaign) the union will make a formal request upon the employer for recognition. Of course the demand may come out of the blue, as the climax of a successful sub rosa campaign. The best union strategy, in earlier years, was to accumulate cards totaling 60 to 70% of the proposed bargaining unit before requesting recognition. More recently, dating from an NLRB policy shift giving greater weight to signed cards as proof of a majority, it has become wiser to seek recognition when a bare majority can be counted.

There are no pat answers the employer can rely on, though. Some organizers in some situations will demand recognition when they have the minimum 30% needed to convince the Board of a "show of interest." And some have been known to go on less, hoping to get to 30% before the Board investigator shows up.

The demand for recognition will be a statement to the employer that the union has a majority of the work force as members, a defini-

(UNION LETTERHEAD)

(Company Name and Address)

Gentlemen:

A substantial majority of Peerless Products employees engaged in production and maintenance operations at the Company's Lake City plant have requested the International Union of _____, AFL-CIO, to represent them as their collective bargaining agency in all matters relating to wages, hours of work and other conditions of employment.

Kindly give us your position in this matter and if agreeable to recognition of the Union as the sole collective bargaining agency for the above described employees, suggest a date for negotiations looking to a collective bargaining agreement.

Very Truly Yours,

International Representative

cc: Regional Director,
    National Labor Relations Board

Figure 2.1. Formal communication from a union.

tion of the work group—proposed bargaining unit—sought and a clear request for bargaining. It may be in the form of a telegram or by word of mouth in a personal visit by the organizer, but it is usually a letter. One company's first formal communication from a labor union is shown in Figure 2.1.

Figure 2.1 is a statement that the union has a majority, and a pass at a description of the proposed bargaining unit (although supervisors would be included in the description). This is no clear request to bargain, only a request for the company's "position." The employer could ignore this letter, with its shortcomings, without risking a refusal-to-bargain charge. The carbon copy for the Regional Director of the NLRB is not unusual but it is gratuitous, since there is no requirement on the union to send it.

The decision to demand recognition is a crucial one for the union, because it represents a point of no return. From here the employer can force an election and if the union fails to win it will not be entitled to another election in that unit for a year, under law. The alternative for the union, if the employer presses for an election that the union does not then want, is an embarrassing "disclaimer of interest."

The demand for recognition will be followed, at a time selected by the union (presuming the employer has not moved for an election), by a petition to the NLRB for an election. The petition is on a form supplied by the NLRB.

In one of the many variations that are possible, the union may forego any formal demand for recognition, with the result that the employer's copy of the petition for an election will be the first notice he has that the union believes it has a majority. (This has been acceptable to the Board in spite of the fact that the petition states that the union has demanded recognition and has been refused.) If there has been no open campaign, the petition may be the first inkling an employer has of the union's existence!

Another common variation on this theme occurs when the employer petitions the NLRB for an election, usually when the union has demanded recognition but does not appear to have a true majority and seems unwilling to go to an election.

NLRB Investigation. The petition for an election will trigger a visit by a representative of the NLRB's Regional Director. He will investigate the union's "show of interest" and whether the employer and the employees being organized are subject to the Labor-Management Relations Act. Satisfying himself that coverage exists, he will determine whether authorization cards are in hand from 30% or more of the proposed bargaining unit. If so, he will attempt to get an agreement from company and union on a "consent election" in which the details—time, place, composition of the bargaining unit, eligible voters—of the election are acceptable to both.

If company and union do not agree on a "consent election," the Regional Director will order a hearing at which the questions will be decided and, if it is warranted, an election will be set. Unless there are serious questions of law or interpretation raised in the hearing, a party can expect no review of the findings; the election will be scheduled at an early date and the next phase of campaigning will begin.

The Pre-Election Phase

The campaigning that takes place when a definite date for an election has been set is similar in many ways to the activity that has occurred in the earlier open campaigning. In those cases where the union has demanded recognition without an open campaign among the employees, the union's attention is almost completely on those employees who are already in its camp. This will be the main emphasis, too, where there has been an open campaign, but there will be some attempt to pick up new supporters.

Labor relations students are familiar with the "Excelsior" case in which the NLRB ruled that an employer must, within seven days after an election is ordered or agreed upon, submit a list of the names and addresses of the eligible voters to the Board for delivery to the union. This places a powerful tool in the hands of the union. It permits the organizer to make mailings to the entire employee group and to make house calls on selected employees whose home addresses otherwise might have to be learned by time consuming inquiry. Home visits are "out of bounds" for the employer.

Unions have been quick to take advantage of the Excelsior rule. Where the union has its 30% "show of interest" but can see the campaign is not going well, some unions will get an election order from the NLRB and will routinely receive the names and addresses of all the employees. The union will then withdraw its election petition. It is prevented from filing another election petition for six months, according to the rules, but the six months can be devoted to every manner of campaigning built around the name-and-address list.

Armed with a list of the addresses of all the eligible voters, the organizers will orient the final campaign toward the election, striving for a peak of interest and enthusiasm on election eve. All stops are pulled. An election eve meeting or party may be held with door prizes and entertainment to stimulate attendance. A "mock election" among the union faithful may be one of the features of the occasion. The atmosphere is like the closing days of a crucial political campaign with an added feature of intense personal pressure on the individual voters.

The activity will seem aimed at the uncommitted group who have supported neither company nor union, but the main thrust of the union effort now is to consolidate and hold the group which has shown an inclination toward the union in the course of the campaigning. The union that cannot, by this time, count enough such supporters to make a majority knows that "No Union" is going to win.

WHY the Union Campaigns

The supervisor must know more than the methods of the union organizer; he must know the considerations that lead the union to his plant in the first place.

where the threat of a strike would carry great weight. Or the union may seek to organize in the other plants of the company only to pre-widely held idea is that the employees are organizing themselves (as the labor laws have it) and the union is only lending limited assistance. That is rarely true. The fact is that, to a well-managed union, organizing is a business. Its organizing campaigns are costed, then funded, just as a businessman plans and finances a new piece of equipment or a project.

A rule of thumb that one union has used is that the cost of organizing should be "paid out" in five years from expected dues, fees and assessments. This is the cost of all organizing, successful and un-successful, so that if a union is successful in one of five campaigns that one success must pay out in one year. One in two successes, or a two-and-a-half year payout would be more typical of the results of NLRB elections, but this is not a good measure. It must be remembered that many organization drives are begun, but are aborted at some point before an election is held.

Unions do not show interest in organizing such groups as sawmill workers, agricultural workers, workers in the service industries or small groups of sales clerks. There are many workers here, but they are on the lower end of the affluence scale and they have little to spare for union dues and fees. They are often widely dispersed geographical-ly, which adds greatly to the expense of organizing activities.

So it is not organizing the unorganized or any other do-good motive that leads the union. It is mostly a matter of money. There are many apparent exceptions to this, but we shall see that over the long run these, too, are usually calculated to add to the unions' income. An ex-ample of this is the organizing drive to "protect jurisdiction." This can occur when a union is recognized by other unions as having general jurisdiction over a certain kind of work, such as a particular craft (e.g., carpenters, retail clerks) or the whole range of work performed in an industry (e.g., rubber workers, communications workers). The union must often do seemingly uneconomic organizing to prevent other unions from organizing within its jurisdiction or to discourage workers within its jurisdiction from working non-union. The target group may be small or unwilling, but in the long run such organizing, too, has a pay-off in that other unions will hesitate to encroach on this jurisdiction and other employers, who otherwise might be able to put up successful resistance, may consider resistance futile and cooperate in the sign-up process. Both make for cheaper organizing.

A second type of uneconomic organizing drive may occur when a union seeks to strengthen its hand in a company with whom it bargains in other localities and the plant or office involved is a key one

Many think the unions go around organizing the unorganized as a sort of idealistic quest. That is almost completely untrue. Another vent its playing the organized groups off against the unorganized ones.

Another non-paying campaign is punitive in nature. It may occur, for example, when a union has been rebuffed in an overture to organize "from the top". (That is, agreeing to a favorable contract with the company before the employees are signed up, or even approached. In return for the "sweetheart" contract, management would tacitly agree to show satisfaction with the union and not to inspect too closely the signed cards that are submitted.) A damaging strike for recognition is often a feature of this kind of campaign. This, too, has a long range payout, as other employers observe the apparent costliness of refusing to make such a deal.

A union may be at the portals because it represents employees in other plants or offices of the company; it may represent other companies in the same industry; it may be strong in a particular locality in other businesses that are somewhat similar; or it may be interested only in a particular craft or skill, whether or not the whole plant or office is engaged in that skill. Each of these represents a special knowledge, angle or gimmick that will enable the union to recruit new members and "service" them at lower cost.

Calculating the payout boils down to gauging the revenues to be expected per unit of campaign cost. Revenues can be equated with the number of employees in the proposed bargaining unit, since for a particular group the dues, fees and assessments are about the same for each person. So, while a sizable working force is preferable, a working force of only two or three can be an economic target if the cost of organizing and servicing is low enough.

The *cost of organizing* is the key factor in a union's decision to undertake a full-scale organizing drive. Many professional organizers feel they can organize any non-union group, given unlimited time and money. So the employer who would remain union-free must take the steps necessary to render his plant, shop or office an uneconomic project to the interested union organizer.

The Union Invests

A well-run union is always on the alert for investment opportunities for its organizing funds and for the services of its staff of organizers (which can also be considered as money, since maintaining a staff of full-time organizers or additional staffers needed to allow time for part-time organizing is a major continuing expense). The expected revenue per new member is predictable. The great variable, and the one the company can and must influence, is the cost per new member.

A union may be asked by a few employees of a firm to come in and organize and be promised a ready-made majority and unions have been known to refuse that request, if it does not appear to be a good business risk! It may even be an acceptable risk, but not the best risk then available to that union and again the employees' request might be refused. Three factors operate to reduce the union income that an employee group will produce:

1. Location in a "right to work" state makes it unlawful for a labor contract to require membership in a union as a condition of remaining employed, so it can be expected that not all of the employees will join and pay dues;

2. The absence of a union dues checkoff provision in a contract makes the collection of dues money by a union infinitely more difficult. This is true only where the contract contains no union shop requirement.

3. Very low pay in the target group leaves little to be expected in the way of dues and assessments.

These factors, generally, are part of the business climate and are not subject to direct control of union or company, but they can be predicted with some accuracy by a union calculating the economics of an organizing drive. So the revenue to be expected is easily known.

The factors that make organizing costly for a union are:

Physical location of the plant or shop. If the union has no local in the same city or area, healthy revenues (many potential members in the bargaining unit) must be available. A union may try to establish a new location on a break-even basis, on the prospect that other workers in the area may be brought into the fold and make a new local a paying operation.

Physical location of the workers who are the target of organizing. The organizer despairs at the thought of a group whose residences are scattered in a rural area, or in the city, a work group whose residences are widely dispersed in different neighborhoods. Either situation presents a difficult house-call communication program.

Community Opposition. Determined opposition to unionization by government, trade associations and business interests of a city can make organizing a hectic, drawn-out pastime, adding up to more dollars spent per new member recruited.

Employee morale and company allegiance. A good attitude on the part of employees tells a union that the company has conducted a successful employee relations program and the effort to make converts of a majority of the group may be too great.

Employer's willingness to defend against unionization strongly and intelligently. Finding that the employer can be expected to wage a strenuous, well-planned campaign of resistance, a union knows organizing costs will be high.

Attitude, ability and preparation of the supervisors. The most important factor is that the employee tends to judge his company and his whole work experience by the words and actions of his supervisor.

Of these, the great variables that in the last analysis make organizing either a profitable or a losing proposition for a union are: (a) the state of mind of the employees, (b) the state of mind of the company, and (c) the state of mind and preparation of the supervisor.

These are the considerations bearing on a union decision to start or continue a campaign. The campaign is then focused almost entirely on the state of mind of the worker as he ultimately finds himself in the privacy of a voting booth with an NLRB ballot in hand.

So in the plant where the two foremen were discussing the organizers' appearance, chances were good that the union would soon be in firm control, not because it was conducting the third stage of a campaign, handbilling the employees openly, but because the foremen were so ignorant of its objectives and methods. One of the foremen had not even had the presence of mind to get one of the handbills. They were not prepared to help their employer resist the union's advances. Many companies will win campaigns in which the union progresses to open campaigning, but not if their foremen are not ready.

Chapter 3
How the Company Defends
Long Range Program

The major company that operates most, or all, of its plants and offices without unions, is not just lucky. Nor is it union-free through choice or oversight on the part of unions. The unions are far too well-run for this. The company has worked at it. These union-free companies, almost without exception, have made a goal of maintaining their freedom and have devoted effort toward reaching it. Their efforts are in the form of planning, organizing, and financing.

A smaller company equally determined to operate without union friction may be less formal in its planning and organizing. Its forces can be gathered and its plans can be executed more swiftly in the event of a union threat. The plans of companies, large and small, are not a list of things to do when the union's organizers appear at the doors. The effective plan begins much sooner.

Most supervisors are familiar with the fireworks and tensions of a union organizing campaign. It is vital that both he and the company are prepared for campaigns. But an even more vital campaign may be carried on when there is no immediate union threat: a cold war that makes the hot organizing campaign a rarity.

The key to this peacetime contest lies in the first phase of the union's expected strategy for organizing the unorganized. This is the exploratory phase the union will go through before it commits men and resources to an expensive active sign-up campaign. Unions usually conduct several explorations before a target is picked, an estimated five or more probes for each full-scale campaign that is started. The efficient union will not accept the poor risks.

The management's counter-strategy here is to do those things over the long run that will make its working people unpromising, expensive targets for the organizer. This is done through a program that operates in the years when no organizers are on the scene. It calls for continuous, committed action by the manager of the union-free office or plant. When the union is knocking on the door it is often too late to begin.

So we have a course of action that is taken long before those moves that counter a union's open organizing drive. If successful, these actions will render the countermeasures unnecessary; an "exploring" union will not choose to go into a full-scale campaign. These same employer actions would have the side effect of developing a more productive, more satisfied work force.

Defensive Plans

Discouraging a union from active campaigning involves, first, self-appraisal in each of several key areas to determine weaknesses and strengths; then establishing priorities and determining the costs of correcting weaknesses and building on strengths. The employer has a wide choice of actions that will improve employee relations. Most of these actions carry a price tag and each such action carries a value in maintaining union-free conditions and in improving productivity. The management's key task is to set priorities, weighing cost and value.

A supervisor may be only faintly aware that the union problem is being studied long before any union is on the horizon. His company, in fact, may have chosen to forego the long-run strategy, as being unneeded. But many union-free companies will have a written, formal plan for remaining free.

The formal plan will, ideally, be in two parts: one program for those periods before a union threat, or between union threats and a double-barreled short range program which is triggered at the time a union is known to be on the scene. A multi-location company will tailor plans for each of its locations. The long range program will be ongoing, emphasizing fact-finding, goal and priority-setting more than specific actions; the short range program will be specific and action-oriented. The long range plan will be concerned with the image of the company in the employee's mind, in his satisfaction with work conditions and his motivation; the short range plan will deal mostly with communicating issues and facts.

The supervisor will normally not be familiar with these plans except as they affect him. Indeed, his company may not have such plans. A long range program is discussed here to underline the importance of the supervisor and to help him in his own planning when he has sole responsibility for a group of employees, he must act alone and no formal plan exists.

The Long Range Program

Typically, a location's long range plan will

1. Identify problem areas.
2. Evaluate the employer's strengths and weaknesses in each of these areas.
3. Set goals for correcting weaknesses and for building on strengths.
4. Establish priorities, perhaps a time schedule, for actions to be taken.

What are the problem areas a plan will consider? It must cover all factors that bear on an employer's ability to discourage a union on the prowl. These may include the business environment, the unions, the employees, the work environment, the needed specific preparations, the pay-benefits-practices situation and training communications.

More positively, a well-conceived and executed plan will not merely discourage, but will repel a union. In some of these areas a searching self-appraisal may become necessary. Action needed and priorities should be dictated by the findings. It is not possible to predict here what actions will be needed; they will be unique to each plant, shop or office.

Here are the more important factors in detail, including the questions that demand answers.

The Business Climate

Are there problems peculiar to the area? Racial, ethnic, population problems? Shortage or oversupply of needed skills? Oddly, a tight labor market makes union organization less likely, presumably because the discontented employee will be able to find work elsewhere and not be inclined to seek a union to help him improve his situation where he is. An exception is a skill in which the unionized work force represents a near-monopoly, as in the heavy construction trades. Community opposition to or sympathy for the union concept? What are the trends in the area for the labor market? Is there a potential wage-hour problem? Equal Employment Opportunities complaint? Workmens Compensation difficulties? Union sympathizers can be expected to blow the whistle on suspected violations of law to show their power to clean up bad conditions. Does the company have prestige in the area? Can local government and police officials be expected to enforce the law in strike situations and other conditions of labor unrest? The employer should never assume that there will be strict enforcement, unless it has been demonstrated in the past. Are the individuals who make up the "labor market" expecting a unionized workplace?

Action a company might take includes taking on community activities to alleviate minority problems, correcting possible technical violations of employment laws, cultivating good relations with local government officials, becoming actively involved in working for good government and tuning hiring practices to meet community responsibilities.

The Union

Taking all the circumstances into account, the company will be able to narrow down to a maximum of two or three the unions who will be interested enough to commit men and money in organizing the company's people and who have some chance of being successful. This finding can be made by learning whether there are

1. Unions in the area that consider the company's operations to be within their jurisdiction.
2. Other unions who are in strength locally and whose philosophy is to "organize the unorganized" without regard to jurisdiction.
3. Unions that represent employees at other locations of the company.
4. Craft unions nearby who have demonstrated an ambition to "carve out" smaller groups of craft employees.
5. Any other unions who may have special reasons for having an interest in your employees.

Regarding the unions isolated as possible opponents: Is there a "track record" of their performance in the general area? What is their preferred modus operandi? A union will usually have a unique style of organizing—techniques, timing of moves, reaction to a company's resistance, attitude toward filing charges with the NLRB. Knowledge of this style gives the target employer a long head start in preparations to resist. What mistakes have they made? Who are their local leaders?

Do you have all the information that is available to the public about these unions? Of special interest here is the wealth of information required to be filed with the government.

1. LM-1 "Labor Organization Information Report". The union must list its initiation fees and dues. Further, copies of its constitution and by-laws are attached and the reporting union must point out the sections that give its provisions for imposing fines and assessments, suspending and expelling members, ratifying contracts and authorizing strikes.

2. LM-2 "Labor Organization Annual Report." In this report the union lists such information as loans receivable from its officers or union members, gifts made by the union, operation of any business, source of receipts, disbursements to each officer and disbursements to each employee which exceeded $10,000 during the year. Here an employer will often find the local organizer's name together with his earnings, expenses and allowances.

3. LM-30. This report is filed by officers and union employees setting forth possible conflicts of interest, such as payments from a consultant or employer, or business dealings with firms that have business with his union.

These documents may be inspected, or copied, through the Department of Labor.

4. The National Labor Relations Board's "NLRB Election Report" is another document of interest. It contains a "box score" of each month's representation elections. The results are grouped within each state by unions.

What is the experience of other nearby employers who bargain with these unions or who have defended against organizing attempts? These employers may have information about union plans or methods for use with your company, identification of key officials and organizers, countermeasures the employers used that were especially effective and the union's general reputation in the area. Can you get copies of its contracts with other employers? It is not unethical to exchange information with other companies about unions and other personnel matters. Other sources of information about unions are local, state and national trade associations, industrial development councils and chambers of commerce. Newspaper files may be helpful.

Many labor relations directors routinely keep a scrapbook of clippings of union action in the city and area—all unions, union officials, violence and threats of violence, strikes, etc. Local and national news of union misbehavior are kept, with an eye toward using photocopies in an organizing campaign, to pursue the theme that all is not perfect in the union way of work life.

The management's action, then, is to prepare itself with the information that will give it an edge when a union comes on the scene.

The Employee

Does the employee "mix" present a problem? Is there national, ethnic or racial imbalance? Very young or very old average age? Out-of-pattern distribution by sex? A long service group or a new plant? Information such as this is important in planning communications and in anticipating the approach the organizer may use.

Have the thought leaders in the employee group been indentified, the people whose opinion the others will follow? Is supervision working on the problem employees: the complainers, the "knockers", the loafers, the mediocrities? Are supervisors studying their people? Is management studying its supervisors?

Is morale high? Are there departments or groups whose morale is noticeably lower than the norm? Tardiness, absenteeism and turnover excessive?

Do the employees really "identify" with the company? Are they motivated and productive? What do they expect from their work life? What do they need?

These are the key questions. Obtaining accurate answers can call for investing money and time in thorough surveys and audits. But this investment may pay out many times over, by trading the shotgun for a rifle in taking corrective actions.

An inquiring organizer will urgently try to get a good "feel" for employee attitudes before launching a campaign. The company is well-nigh impregnable if his opinion sample leaves his ears ringing with phrases such as:

"The company will keep finding ways to provide steady work . . . the gang likes to have me around; I am treated like a man . . . we get credit and thanks from topside when we have earned it . . . they do their best to make this a respectable place to work . . . it's safe, pleasant, healthy and friendly . . . they recognize long service and provide decent benefits . . . they promote from within and there are always places for those who want to get ahead and will 'put out' . . . I'll have a good future if the company has a good future . . . my skill and ideas are recognized. . . .

"Our pay is as good as anybody gets for the same kind of work around here . . . there's nothing routine about my job—it keeps me thinking and I like it . . . if the company makes a good profit I am sure we will share in it somehow . . . the top brass are a good bunch of joes. They are honest, hard-working, capable men who shoot straight and they will think about us in any decision they make . . . we turn out a good product here and we have to keep up our good reputation . . . my foreman knows what he is doing; he is fair, friendly and helps when needed . . . I am told how I am doing, where I fit in and what is going on . . . when I have an idea they listen to it . . . they depend on us for good, fast work. . . ."

The organizer will type a report telling the union's director of education he wouldn't touch this group with a ten-foot pole.

Weeding Out Undesirables

Corrective action by the company might be long-term upgrading of the employee group by ridding itself of problem employees who cannot be salvaged:

The value of upgrading a work force by a "pruning" process is recognized on both sides. The following statement is attributed only to "an old organizer" who is giving advice to management, based on his organizing experience:

Sometimes we union people are amazed at how naive company officers are when it comes to dealing with people and unions.

To begin with, I make little headway in my efforts to organize a plant, store or any other establishment in which the employees are happy, where they are doing a good job, and where they are treated with fair and thoughtful consideration. It can rarely be done. Let me tell you what I would do if I were the owner or manager of an establishment and I wanted to insure myself against a union.

First, I would discharge every employee that I had who was doing a poor and unsatisfactory job. We union organizers always start a drive with the disgruntled worker, the one that shirks his responsibilities, the loafer—the employee that management has really meant to discharge for the past several months but for some reason hasn't. That is the kind of employee that I look for. I can't interest employees in a union who are happy conscientious workers.

The inefficient worker knows that he is a chiseler and looks for someone to blame besides himself. Very shortly he is finding fault with his foreman, his supervisor or his plant manager and when he gets no consolation from within the plant he turns to a source outside the plant, or, in other words, to a union organizer.

So, my first advice to industry would be to discharge immediately every poor and inefficient worker in the plant. Don't wait. *Do it now before it is too late!*

Finally, if I did not want a union, I would make a policy to tell employees something about the economic condition of the company. They like to know how business is, where the organization is going, whether they will have steady work for the next six months. Only in that way can they make their own plans—plans about a new car, a new home, or sending their children to college.

The company will set goals in the matter of its hiring practices. Management should be reasonably certain, at the minimum, that it is not hiring a union "plant" whose purpose is to organize from within. Ideally, the employment program will recruit people who are apt to be pro-company in an organizing campaign (though this quality in a prospective employee is hard to pin down).

More importantly the company must have the high-quality leaders that provide the atmosphere for self-motivation and productivity, the challenging and worthwhile jobs, the feeling that the individual counts for something and the understanding and support.

The Work Environment

There is no absolute standard of physical comfort for a place of work that an employer can rely upon. To the worker it is more a question of whether the employer is doing what he reasonably can do to provide comfort at work. Is lighting sufficient? Ventilation good? If air-conditioned, is the system well regulated? Floors and walls clean and well-maintained? Especially, are the washrooms, locker rooms and sanitary facilities clean and attractive? Is there a good place to eat? Is there a noise, smell or fume problem? Are the employees being asked to work too much overtime? Is parking convenient? Is irritating special privilege given to higher-ups in parking, working hours and other conspicuous incidentals?

At least as important as the physical work setting is the structure of the jobs the company offers. Does each job bring a challenge or does it tend to be repetitive, dull and monotonous? Building stimulating jobs within our mechanized, efficient technology is an ever-growing problem for supervisor and manager alike.

The Specific Preparations

One element of the company's long range plan that involves very little fact-finding is the specific action it must take to place itself in a favorable posture to oppose a union campaign. A check list of these might read as follows:

Protection against "carve-out." Among the more important powers of the NLRB is its ability to name an "appropriate bargaining unit." This unit may well be only a portion of the plant or office, if it can be regarded with some logic as a separate group. Many unions will concentrate their efforts on a single craft or type of worker and attempt to secure an election only among them ("carve them out" of the bigger group, in the common expression). To prevent this a company will structure its jobs and work groups so that the conventional construction crafts do not work as separate units; the operation people also maintain equipment; the clerical people are given diversification and decision-making responsibilities.

Besides making a carve-out more difficult, this can be a more efficient way to operate.

Establishment of a lawful solicitation rule. Under ordinary circumstances an employer is entitled to have a rule forbidding non-employee organizers to come on company property and forbidding employees to solicit other employees during working time or to distribute literature any time in work areas. "Work time" means most of the work day except times such as coffee breaks, lunch hour or clock-out waiting. The following is a statement of such a rule for employees:

> Posting of notices and other written material on company property is not permitted without prior written approval of the supervisor in charge. Circulation or distribution of printed material of any type in any work area or in any area on employee's work time and solicitation of employees on their work time are prohibited. Superior ordinarily endorses only one solicitation per year that being the local United Fund drive or its equivalent.

It is a good idea to specify the solicitations that will be permitted. The NLRB position, not upheld always by the courts, is that the rule may not be directed specifically at union organizing nor be enforced only against union organization. In day-to-day operation, then, the company must see that its no solicitation rule is evenly enforced to be sure it is available when the union comes around. This means no more Girl Scout cookie selling, collecting get-well gift funds or local politicking.

Keeping short range resistance plans updated. The short range program will usually establish a special organization for the task of defending against a union's active campaign. This organization must be kept current as personnel changes occur over a period of time. The plan itself should be reviewed regularly in the light of changing conditions, laws and organizing tactics.

Maintaining legal counsel. Legal counsel for the active campaign should not be a last minute selection. The lawyer or firm should be selected for ability to handle labor relations matters; this is not an automatic additional assignment for the firm's regular legal counsel. Good relationships should be cultivated with counsel and unique problems that can be foreseen should be discussed in advance.

Readiness of service employees. In its eagerness to train employees, supervisors and middle management people the company should not overlook its service personnel. Their role can be crucial. One large union-free company gives high importance to the personality, attitude and communicating ability of applicants being screened for the position of plant nurse. Those employed are alerted to the company's need for accurate news of employee gripes and worries, poor working conditions and the presence of union organizers on the scene. All service employees who come into contact with the workers must be on the look-out for dissatisfying factors on the work scene. Reporting findings should be a regular task of people such as the safety engineers, guards, plant clerks, timekeepers and inspectors.

Policies and practices booklet. Almost without exception the larger non-union plants and offices publish employee handbooks. It makes sense for a number of reasons. Manuals of policy and practice were once considered practical only in the larger groups. In small locations it was felt that workers would know the benefits and rules, due to closer contact with supervision. Also the cost of printing, per person, seemed unreasonable.

The trend now is toward giving handbooks to the small group. The employee has the satisfaction of seeing his "deal" with the company in writing (the closer contact of the small location does not do a good job of communicating this kind of information). Costs need not be high, since the manual does not have to be a slick paper production or even set in type, when today's offset printing techniques are used.

Handbooks are effective in giving an exact statement of the benefits offered, and in presenting the work rules and the "shalt nots" in a wholesome manner. But it is as a union-defense tool that handbooks are most useful. One of the main reasons for voting for a union, according to workers, is they have been promised a contract that will assure them of their benefits and rights. Unions do not fail to stress this in their campaigns. A good policy and practice manual washes it out as an argument.

The handbook is also the appropriate place to set forth the "no solicitation" rule as it applies to employees.

Physical security. The number and the placement of entries to the plant or office may be key factors in defending against a union organizer's efforts. For example, when there is a construction job underway at the site, it is standard practice to set up a separate gate and clock alley for the construction group. This insulates the company's workers from the turmoil of union activity among construction workers (this is done even though the company's people be unionized). There will often be a separate gate for each contractor and sub-contractor who is on the job; sometimes a gate for each separate union. In this posture a picket line of one group will not paralyse the whole job and the plant's operation.

A second purpose to be served by careful planning of physical layout is minimum exposure to outside, non-employee, union solicitors. Where it is practical, multiple entrances to work prevent funneling employees past one spot, easy targets for solicitation. In most cases, solicitors (whether union or advertiser) may be excluded from company property. Thus, where a company parking lot lies between the public street and the actual entrance to the workplace, it is wise, again, to have several entrances to the parking.

Some employers provide many, well-scattered drinking fountains and more, smaller washrooms to discourage large informal gatherings. This is done to reduce the time away from work and to dampen the spread of rumors, but it also helps to block inside (employee) solicitation for a union.

Pay, Benefits and Work Practices

Wages

Adequate wage levels are basic in the company's long-term maintenance of positive employee feelings. Pay has its greatest importance in a negative way; less than adequate pay can cause great dissatisfaction, but adding more and more pay above adequate levels does not add proportionately to satisfaction.

The company's toughest problem in this area is knowing what "adequate" wages are. As with working conditions, there is no absolute scale that can be followed. In each plant, shop or office the optimum wage level is that level which meets the expectations of the employees but what the employees expect can seldom be determined with precision. They will have some knowledge of such factors as the local wage level for generally comparable work; the general wage levels in the same industries in the region; the pay being received by their friends and neighbors; the movement of local and national cost of living indices; and the actual needs they feel in terms of pay.

The union-free management will usually key on local pay for the industry or for the type of work. The union will be able, often, to point out higher pay in distant places, but the employee does not identify so easily with workers elsewhere.

Another facet of employee satisfaction with pay is the company's method for setting rates of pay for the particular job and for individual employees. Errors here can create dissatisfaction, even though the general level of pay is beyond reproach.

One approach to solving both of these problems is to involve the employees in research into the rates paid in the industry and area and to study the system for setting individual rates. A committee of employee leaders could be appointed for this purpose. There are many ways to go about it, but some type of "listening" device to sample employee opinion on wages is a *must*.

Are continuing studies of area and industry pay rates carried on? Is the system for establishing pay levels and setting individual pay fully understood by each employee? Is merit in performance of the job considered in setting a person's pay rate? Are overtime, premium, and penalty pay practices in line? Countless miscellaneous pay practices fall under this heading. These include premium payments for time worked: on holidays, over a stated number of hours in a week or a day or in succession, on a Saturday or Sunday, on rotating shifts, on a call-in for emergency work, for specified hazardous work, etc. Another example is paying a fixed amount for or providing a meal when a worker is held over beyond his normal meal time to do extra work.

Study must also be made of local practices in the various types of pay for time *not* worked—vacations, holidays, paid leaves of absence for such events as funeral in the family, jury duty and urgent personal business. Like pay rates, these practices should conform to the workers' expectations, which in turn are formed most often from their experience with local patterns. The employer is well advised, then, to stay in touch with the practices of the local competition, and with his employees' opinions on the subject.

Health Plans

Hospital, medical and sick pay plans also must be held at adequate levels—once again, *adequate* in the minds of the employees. Local standards for health plans are of much greater importance than industry and national standards. Notably, too, in this kind of benefit the union-free employer will often deliberately go well beyond the adequate level, since at moderate extra cost these adequate-plus dollars will be paid out at times when they are most needed and appreciated.

The employer will systematically audit the performance of his various disability benefit plans. Again, a continuing sample of employee opinion is needed. Are the benefits administered in an intelligent manner? An otherwise generous health plan can generate dissatisfaction. Employees can be irritated and frustrated by an excess of red tape, over-long claim forms and delayed payments (due, perhaps, to overzealous review of claims—hardly necessary where discipline can be freely imposed for abuse of the plan). Poor communication of the details of the plans can cause morale problems by allowing employees to believe they are entitled to benefits that do not exist (then being disappointed when a claim is denied.) Are the benefits easy to apply for, and are they paid promptly? Does the employee have the feeling that his word is trusted?

Pension Plans and Savings Plans

Pension plans and other long term savings plans, though certainly deserving a place in the balanced employee relations program, have little importance in the long- or short-term resistance to union organization. They have no clout as an issue for an organizer unless they are woefully inadequate, or the work force is woefully aged.

Seniority

Management, in the time before an active union organizing drive, should assure itself that a consistent policy on seniority is being followed. Seniority is a classic rallying point of the union organizer. The employer can easily remove this issue by going to a strict seniority system, but in doing this he would give away one of the great advantages of operating without a union. The ability to advance and assign people scientifically gives management an opportunity to upgrade its work force. From the employee viewpoint this right to promote provides the natural reward for people of top talent, motivation and potential.

On the other hand, the employer must recognize a responsibility to the working man who has dedicated years of his life to the business and is fitted for no other work. This may not be due to any fault of the man, only to the specialized nature of the jobs he has held. The employer must recognize that even in those crafts and trades that have a wider market, the use of seniority at other places of employment restricts a man's ability to move freely between employers.

The employer should recognize, too, that the typical promotion in the lower jobs is not often critical; there are usually a number of people qualified or easily trained to qualify to advance. The most senior man is usually qualified for the advancement. This is the nub of the problem: management may know who is the best qualified man and he is one with lesser seniority. It is suggested that the less senior man should be advanced only when his superior ability is recognized by all. The whole work group feels involved in any single promotion and negative feelings of the group, feelings of injustice, can offset any improved productivity that appointment of a slightly better qualified, but less senior, man would bring.

Layoffs? When layoffs become necessary, it has been suggested that the other tack be followed—lay off by seniority (opinion is divided here, many personnel people holding that this decision is even more important than promotion and should be made on a merit basis). Such matters as choice of an open job where there is no productivity question, choice of vacation period, choice of shift? Strict seniority.

Transfers and Assignments

The ability to transfer employees to jobs they can do best and the freedom to assign overtime work to fully-qualified people is another management opportunity to enhance productivity. Seniority should be observed where efficiency will not be affected in a transfer. A systematic way of distributing overtime fairly should be observed, always with provision for the special situation when a particular person is needed or where people who have brought a job near completion can be used whenever a "holdover" is necessary.

Complaint Handling

A written procedure for the handling of employee complaints and grievances is basic in most large union-free plants or offices. Many employers who have grievance procedures in union-free locations have observed that the procedure, however cleverly planned, hasn't been used a lot. This is not all bad, though it would be better to know that all complaints are out on the table and are being settled. The mere fact that the procedure is there does much to prevent feelings of dissatisfaction. And it removes a favorite union issue.

Making it easy to use, and encouraging employees to use it should be part of the planning for a new grievance procedure.

The foreman need not wait for his company to install a grievance procedure. He can go right ahead in the area under his control. He can do this by making it clear to his people that one of his important duties is to accept job-connected complaints and try to straighten them out and that if he and the employee cannot agree on the answer, the employee is entitled to appeal to a member of higher management either orally or in writing (this will be a person who has agreed to serve in this capacity). Then he must be truly receptive to complaints.

Crude? Yes, but far better than no grievance handling plan at all.

Discipline

The whole subject of discipline cries for the employer's attention before a union becomes interested. Whatever rules of behavior the company chooses to establish should be fully known to all. Assuring that this has been done and determining what the rules should be—indeed, what the company's whole approach to discipline should be—are management's concern in a long range plan. An employee handbook statement on discipline might read like this:

It is basic in our personnel relations that the purpose of disciplinary action is to correct the offender's behavior, if possible, not to punish. The penalty of discharge shall be resorted to only when other discipline is useless after appropriate warning has been given. An exception is the offense that in itself is sufficiently serious to merit discharge without a specific prior warning. Generally, this is an offense that involves disregard of your own and others' safety or the security of company property.

There is growing belief that discipline in the union-free work force should be approached on a self-policing basis: a basis not possible in a unionized situation where mechanical, strict enforcement must be the rule. This new approach starts from the assumption that each employee accepts the existing rules and is ready to take the responsibility of living by them. Infractions are met with a sincere attempt to understand the offender's motives and private counseling with him. The employee is led to set goals for himself in the matter of observing the rules. The counseling takes place at higher levels if infractions persist. There is, in effect, no discipline except that of discharge, and that only for unredeemable cases. These turn out to be extremely rare.

This or any other approach to discipline is not for the foreman or supervisor to introduce independently as he may in the case of a grievance procedure. Discipline must be evenly dealt out in all departments.

New ideas

The old customs in pay and work rules are always open to challenge by fresh approaches. An alert company sifts the new ideas carefully. Being among the first to adopt a new technique reflects a genuine concern for the well-being of employees as opposed to the image of a company which will change only after being overwhelmed by a pattern all about it.

For example, who says the pay for a particular hourly paid job should be the same for all who perform this job, from the newest recruit and the marginal performer to the most skilled, motivated and productive people? At least one union-free company establishes a range within which each employee is paid for a job. This level is based on performance, not on merit which implies personal merit rather than the only tenable standards of ability and output at work. There is danger of favoritism creeping into such a system, however, and it is not recommended for use without the credible and uncomplicated appraisal system that must go with it. Let's look at some others:

Salary vs. Hourly Pay. Why should certain occupations be paid by the hour, rather than by salary? It makes for somewhat easier "distribution" of direct labor costs, especially in the maintenance or small-lot production functions. It simplifies payroll calculations where overtime is involved. But many companies are breaking away from paying their people by the hour of work. The Fair Labor Standards Act does not require that non-exempt people be paid in this manner. The union-free employer has enough control of performance and attendance standards to assure that a salaried payroll, with its implication of a guaranteed wage, presents no problem of malingering. In the future it may be considered demeaning to pay a human being by the hour.

The Disappearing Time Clock. A large number of companies who still have an hourly payroll no longer require each worker to punch a time card in and out of work. Time cards are not required by law and are only a supplement to payroll accounting. The mechanical approach to employment that the time clock reflects is no longer thought to be consonant with good employee relations.

The Short Work Week. A hot new idea in employment today is the breakout from the standard five-day, 40-hour work week. The companies experimenting with a shorter week tend to be smaller companies who feel they can compete with the majors for the better employees by offering a better work schedule. There is no one system; the plan may be four ten-hour days, the week may be less than forty hours; and a three-day, 12-hour plan has been tried.

Most employees love it. They appreciate the leisure and find there is seldom need to lay off from work to tend to small items of personal business. Some companies have experienced loss of productivity, increased moonlighting and find they can not afford to be unmanned. But much company experience to date has been favorable. The short work week may be a powerful tool for the smaller company.

Flexible Work Hours. Showing even more promise than the short work week is the concept of the flexible work day, wherein workers choose their own starting and quitting times, in fact being required to be present at work only during named "core hours." Core hours are, generally, the five or six hours about the middle of the day when the entire work force will be present. There are many versions of this plan but the one basic is that the individual is allowed to arrange his own schedule.

Part-Time Worker. Akin to the flexible work hours idea is the employment of people on a regular part-time basis. This is found, typically, where female workers are involved and jobs can be split between two who for personal reasons cannot work the full day. Organizers consider this kind of worker difficult to convert to unionism.

Shift Schedule Innovations. Where the plant must operate around the clock there is typically an arrangement in which workers rotate through each of the shifts, changing weekly. Recent research findings indicate this may be injurious to health, since it now appears that most people require about three weeks to adapt to a new eating-sleeping cycle. It has been suggested that a combination schedule be adopted: a fixed midnight shift (which some workers prefer in any case) and a rotating evening and day shift (combining the prized day shift with the unpopular evening shift). This would give all workers an unchanging eat-sleep schedule.

Communications Training

The communication and training activities in the long range program of the large employer are well classified as "specific preparations." They are almost invariably present in the programs of the large union-free companies.

An in-depth study of nearly 650 elections which resulted in union victories indicated there were five major employer errors, alone or in combination, which led to the employer's loss:

1. Gave the employees only a minimum of feedback on the company's health: its financial position, its goals, sales and production accomplishments.
2. Made important changes in plant equipment, tooling or policies without advance notice or later explanation to the work force.
3. Made key decisions affecting the employees in a vacuum of ignorance about what the employees really wanted.
4. Used driving and pressure tactics rather than leadership to secure high production and productivity.

5. Minimized or refused to believe employee dissatisfaction at the workplace.

Four of the five are failures of communication.

The employer must act, over the long run, to establish credibility and to set up credible channels of communication with the employees; he must be disposed to communicate the work-connected news, good or bad. Not just one channel will be developed in the larger plants and offices, but a variety:

Use of letters to the homes of employees for major announcements. The union will deride a sudden show of interest around election time, it is far better to establish a practice of sharing important news in this manner through the years.

Sponsoring a newsy, quick-hitting newspaper or news-letter to transmit less crucial announcements and to convey opinion and comment, along with specific news of employee activities and personal items. The trend is to offer more news of company business moves and financial data. News of the situations where the employees are getting a better deal than their unionized counterparts is frankly published.

Cultivating as many personal contacts as possible in the working force by as many executives and managers as possible within the limitations of their available time. This is done mainly by visits to the workplace on a regular basis, by attendance at employee functions and by cultivating other outside-work contacts.

Finding occasions to hold large meetings of employees on company time, the forerunner of the well-known "captive audience" speech. One version of such a meeting is a simulated stockholder meeting for the employees.

Using innovative approaches:

1. One company holds monthly meetings of small groups of employees with a member of higher management encouraging free discussion. The meetings have continued through two union organization attempts, both lost by the union with no charge of law-breaking raised.

2. Many companies are using their video tape monitors in lunchrooms and lounges to pass information about company benefit plans, products, financial condition, safety tips and the like. A program may be run over and over during leisure time on a 'closed loop.' Many of the programs are designed to 'star' local workers and supervisors.

3. It has become almost the rule, rather than the exception, for larger plants to have "hot line" telephones, which employees and supervisors can dial to pick up a recorded message. The message can deliver news up-to-the-minute.

Blocking Unwanted Communication

The company must also move to make it harder for outsiders to communicate with employees. To this end employee name and address lists are kept confidential (a good idea, anyway, to keep such lists out of the hands of advertisers). Easing traffic flow at plant gates prevents massing into groups easy to solicit and ends the irritation of standing in line.

This by no means discharges the management's communication responsibilities. To this point the most effective tools of all, the direct contact between worker and supervisor, and the entire area of upward communication have not been discussed. These are training responsibilities of the management, unless its self-audit can give assurance that such training is not needed.

The supervisor must have sharp person-to-person communicating skills and he must know his responsibility as the vital connecting link in upward communication, in the "feedback." Supervisors must have specific training in the requirements of the law of union organizing, as it relates to them. They must be trained in the techniques of supervision that will contribute toward keeping the workplace union-free.

Training must also be brought direct to the employee. The management must assure itself that each of its employees knows the function of the plant or office, the company's products and service, the business problems, the organization, the principal customers and competitors. Each should know something of the management's philosophy including, of course, its position on unionization.

The new employee should be greeted with the company's policy on unionized operation early in his induction-orientation. This means a clear statement such as this by the highest official available:

This meeting is to let you know Superior's position and views on labor unionism.

We do not say that unionism itself is either good or bad. We do say that here, at this time, we judge that Superior will have a happier, more secure and stable place to work if we continue to operate without a union handling the relations between you and us.

This may sound like Superior is anti-union. Not so. Superior has operated plants and offices all over the nation with unions;

at the same time we operate plants and offices without unions. But if we are not anti-union, we *are* pro-Superior. We want to maintain our way of working together because it makes this location more productive and profitable and more likely to be in operation for a long time. It makes strikes impossible and, all the way around, it is a better place to work when we are all pulling together.

From your point of view, you will share the security that profitable operation brings. You will never suffer the loss of pay and the bitterness and hatred caused by strikes. Again, for you it is a more satisfying place to work when we are working as a team.

You pay nothing to work for' Superior, but the cost of unionism can be high. In addition to dues, fees and special assessments there may be costly strikes and lower production which will make your job less secure.

Those among you who have worked in both union and non-union situations can tell you this is true.

And so it is that we try our best to give you fair pay, an important job, a pleasant place to work, a good supervisor and, finally, the opportunity to advance as far as your own ability will permit. Your job is as secure as you make it. We think you are entitled to all of these and if you don't think you are getting them, we want to hear from you about it.

Working together like this, there is no limit to what we can do!

Conclusion

These are the factors which may appear in a full-scale long range program of a company to remain union-free. They are those parts of a total company employee-community relations program that bear directly on the company's exposure to unionism. Some of them have no application in certain situations; others not mentioned here may need to be part of a location's plan. Some are less important than others: usually the business environment and the union information will not compete in importance with the factors that relate to the employees, the specific preparations, benefits, work practices, training and communications. Failure in the areas of pay, benefits, work practices and work conditions will cancel superlative efforts in other areas.

The program has no set form but, in some manner, goals must be set and actions must be outlined in those areas that need attention.

The total goal is a work force and an environment that will totally discourage union organizing.

Chapter 4
How the Company Defends
Short Range Program

The long range program doesn't always succeed in killing the union's interest. For those companies that have long range plans and those who don't, a second type of program is needed: a plan for a counter-campaign.

Is there a chance for success? Can a company hope to hold off a full-scale organizing campaign by a union? NLRB summaries of the results of elections show that today just under half of them are lost by the union. These are not bad odds for the employer, but remember too, in each election the union thought it would win or there would not have been an election. Many of the union wins occur when the employer does not actively oppose the union. This happens when the employer has asked a "sweetheart" union to go through the motions of getting a certification or when the employer believes it futile to resist. Unions win more than 90% of elections in which they are not resisted.

Crank into the equation the fact that many campaigns are halted short of an election by the union or never seriously started due to lack of success and the employer's chance look even better. It is estimated that five approaches are made by unions for every one that goes on to an election. Then only half are winners, as we have seen.

Organizing Problems

The better odds now enjoyed by the employer are attributed to problems facing the union organizer that have been growing in recent years. These problems are the areas of a) the present-day work scene,

b) the new employee mix, c) union top leadership and d) management action.

The New Work Scene

Plant and shop jobs are declining as a percent of total work force, victims of new technology. These were the strongholds of the unions. The knowledge workers and clerical workers coming on the scene are not union-oriented.

High wages and better working conditions are not the preserve of union employment. Union-free people are as well off as their colleagues in the union shops and are free of union dues and work interruptions as well. Today's prosperous work force is frightened by labor's history of violence. Employees are not so anxious to strike and union-free employees not so willing to assume the risk of strikes and similar activity that a union can bring.

The "class struggle" as an issue is dead. Unions have not fully learned this lesson if we can judge by their propaganda which is too heavy-handed and abusive of the bosses for the more sophisticated workers of today.

The New Employee Mix

The number of white collar and technical employees is increasing rapidly and the organizers have not found the key to enrolling these types in large groups. The shift of industry to new regions of the nation has brought a new type of employee to the work force, one who has not had a tradition of unionism. This may be an understatement: to many of them the idea is flatly repugnant. It has also been observed that people transferring from organized plants to plants in the new areas often reject unionism in the new climate.

Union Leadership

Top union leadership is accused of being outdated, still fighting the battles of the Depression. Few employees today can remember the Depression. The old line leadership is deeply entrenched and it tends to support causes that do not concern the grass roots membership. Potential new members are turned away by this. Crusading young people no longer look upon a career in union leadership as being one of service. Labor is no longer the underdog. Many other doors are open to the young idealist.

The "image" cf top union leadership, whether deserved or not, has hurt the organizers. Wide publicity given corruption, gangster tactics and "public be damned" attitude on the part of a few leaders has changed the public's attitude toward union leaders as a group.

Management Action

Management no longer pulls its punches on the union issue. Its wages, fringes, policies and practices are usually fair and it doesn't hesitate to take its case to the public and to the employee. Management doesn't press the panic button when a union appears. It knows how to conduct a counter-campaign. Supervisors are better prepared to pull their weight in the campaign.

The Plan

Many companies do not have a specific short range program ready at all times. Personal know-how and flexibility can accomplish the same purpose. This discussion will embrace all of the subjects of planning that seem of general interest. A plan will not necessarily include all of these; it should in fact include only those important in the local situation.

The short range program is triggered at the first knowledge that a union is attempting to organize the company's employees. This plan ideally will be in two main parts: a program that operates while the union is working underground and a program that starts up when the union's campaign first comes into the open by open soliciting, by a demand upon management for recognition, by an election petition to the NLRB or by any action which clearly exposes its presence.

The first step after the union's drive has been detected is to put aside any long range resistance plans and organize for the short range. This means breathing life into the organization which will conduct the company's counter-campaign. A good long range plan will have set up and have kept this organization current. The regular organization of a large plant or office, while adequate to handle a long range plan, is rarely prepared to take over the management of an active short range campaign.

Perhaps the best organization for this purpose, at least in the large company, is a task force or a committee with a powerful chairman—one person with sweeping authority. He will have restraints, of course, in the form of having to clear certain actions with higher-ups. Higher management will usually retain the duty of assuring the legality of company action and will have a hand in determining the company's posture or image and in setting the "tone" of the campaign.

Some large companies will dispatch staff people from headquarters to take charge of the campaign. A labor relations consultant may be called upon to head the campaign or to work with the group or person heading the campaign. Legal firms are available which make a specialty of fending off union organizing attempts. It is most desirable that the consultant or law firm be chosen in "peacetime" so they may be familiar with the problems that may arise and with the people with whom they must work.

In the smaller workplace, an individual may be given the job of heading the counter-campaign or, most often, the manager will take on the responsibility himself. Whether it is a task force, law firm or one-man show, the crucial areas should be staffed by the best talent available. These areas are communication, fact-gathering, training and public-community relations.

Decisions Needed: Sub Rosa Phase

At the outset the campaign leadership will be largely involved with decision-making. Good information is vital. All feedback about the union's organizing moves and employee attitudes and opinion will funnel to one clearly defined center. Regular meetings of the campaign organization and others who have, or need, information will be firmly scheduled. These meetings will evaluate the progress of both the company and union campaigns. To this end, it is a good idea to keep a daily record of reported union activity and of all known personal contacts by union representatives with employees.

The urgent need for early warning of union activity is underlined by a look at the many decisions best made and actions best taken before the union's campaign is in the open. A firm schedule of company action cannot yet be made, because the period of time available is not known. It is still hoped that the union will not find the terrain to its liking and withdraw. Union activity may seem to decrease or come to a stop for days or weeks at a time. This is usually due to the organizers having other irons in the fire.

Before the union's campaign surfaces, the campaign leadership must busy itself in the areas of overall strategy, fence-mending (perhaps), certain preparations and training. It is most awkward when there is no warning and these activities must be sandwiched into a hectic campaign.

Strategy

When the union is discovered to be quietly active, a vital decision must be made whether a) to accomplish (on a basis that does not acknowledge existence of the union's activity) corrections in conditions that are causing dissatisfaction and take other actions in the nature of fence-mending, or b) to commence immediately to communicate with employees on the importance of not signing the authorization cards the union is pushing or which are being "sold" to them, perhaps, as merely a request for a secret ballot election. The latter is a new side of management strategy made necessary by the NLRB's recent readiness to rely on authorization cards as proof of a majority. It forecloses most fence-mending activity.

If the decision is to communicate, another decision is needed whether to communicate quietly through the supervisors, whether to communicate direct from management on an informational basis, or whether to go all-out in a counter-drive to resist card signing.

The leadership must define the issues and must decide which members of management will be spotlighted in any open campaign: who will make the statements and write the letters, whether the company will be "personalized" in one individual and who will be given a "low profile."

The soundness of these decisions depends utterly on having accurate information about the seriousness of the union's intentions and the success the union is having.

Fence Mending

In the period before the union's campaign is public knowledge the company has a last chance to improve pay, benefits and working conditions without serious danger of violating the law and *no* danger of running afoul of the NLRB's election rules. "Fence mending" here means completing actions that are already in the works in response to needs that have been recognized. And if the feedback reveals sources of employee dissatisfaction that had not been known before, there may still be time during the union's sub rosa drive to get a start on these problems.

Another very ticklish situation is removing "problem" employees. Even in the confidential stage of a union campaign an employee may not and, morally, should not be discharged or disciplined for his union activity, but after an open campaign is under way it is difficult to remove problem employees for any reason without risk of its being claimed to be for their unionism. A discharge is a ready-made "cause" for the union. A discharge will be protested to the NLRB where other actions, more helpful in defeating the union, might not.

Finally, in clearing the decks for action the employer must look to his lower management and supervision and neutralize those individuals who may be liabilities in a hot campaign. This is done by such measures as counseling and instruction and, if necessary, by transfers and shifting of duties.

Specific Preparations

The campaign leadership should gather all available information about the union that is working among the employees. The leaders can learn the experiences of other employers with the union, both in organizing and negotiating, get copies of contracts the union has signed with other companies, become familiar with its organizing methods and personnel, see if local trade associations have information to contribute and get the information that is public in government files.

The company's position should be hammered out and agreed upon or cleared at higher levels on all the issues that are known or expected to be brought up by the union. Facts should be documented. Rapid means of publishing letters, posters and handouts must be arranged. Mailing lists must be updated, perhaps several "decks" of addressed envelopes should be prepared, if no automatic addressing system is available. Deadlines for posting, to get letters to employees' homes on a given day, should be learned.

Information Gathering

Reports filtering back from employees via the supervisors are the chief source of news of the campaign's progress (campaign leadership is always alert for the "planted" story or "sandbagging"). The campaign heads should also use any other channel that is available: employers who already bargain with the organizing union are excellent sources of the union's activity; contacts within the local union movement are valuable.

Training

Supervisors and security forces will be rehearsed on the limits of their legal activity and communication. The telephone switchboard people and receptionists will be alerted to handling the call or visit of an organizer. Security personnel will be drilled in their responsibility for enforcing the rules on solicitation and handbill distribution. Communicating will be featured in the training given supervisors.

Supervisors will be instructed to be alert for news of the campaign and to be aware of the need and the channel for feeding back any information they gather to campaign G.H.Q. Every item of news must be passed along regardless of its seeming unimportance.

All management, supervisors and security people must be taught what to expect in a union organizing drive. In the early part of the sub rosa stage the union's exploration phase is complete. The remainder of the campaign is usually discussed in two parts: the open campaigning before an election is scheduled and the union's campaigning that goes on just before the election. There may be some value in recognizing an "in-between" phase: the short period when a demand for recognition has been made or petition for an election has been sent to the NLRB, but the election has not been scheduled. In this short time the union's tactics change, because it is for the first time committed to carry on.

Management Strategy Shift

It should be pointed out that the scope of management action changes with the different parts of the union campaign. For most practical purposes the company's campaigning can be divided into the period before the union is in the open and the period after the union is in the open. Past the dividing point, for instance, the company can no longer engage freely in fence-mending activities; the supervisor may no longer call an employee into his office to talk about unionism; a member of management may no longer make home calls on employees relating to unionism. Company campaigning that is done after the union is in the open changes slightly through the different stages in respect to demands of the law and the NLRB's rules; this affects the content of the counter-campaign but does not slow down the campaign itself.

In outlining the expected actions of the union for supervisors and security people, it is urgent to point out that these stages are *possible* but the unexpected is more likely:

1. A demand for election and an election petition to the Board may be the first notice an employer has that a campaign is in progress. This eliminates the open-period-before-petition stage. It can happen when a union cuts the preparatory period very short or—this is a sure indicator of trouble—when the company's upward communication has failed to give notice of an extensive sub rosa campaign. Supervision and security people must be reminded not to acknowledge a demand for recognition, written or word-of-mouth, or to accept any proof of a majority a union representative may tender. Matters such as these must be referred to the location manager or the person designated by the campaign leadership.

2. A demand for recognition may ask for a privately held election and if for some reason this is accepted by management there will be no petition to the Board. A demand like this, when refused, has often proved to be the end of the campaign: The union judges it cannot go forward with the expense of a campaign and formal election.

3. There may be no demand for recognition, only a petition to the Board.

4. There may be no public activity by the union, even after an election is scheduled. This is a signal that the union has a safe majority and is "standing pat", relying on home visits and person-to-person talks to hold its own.

The assumption here is that the union will attempt to be bargaining agent through the election process. In actual practice the union may attempt to force recognition by calling its people out on strike.

So the importance of detecting union preliminary activities cannot be over-stressed in training supervisors. Such activities are seldom omitted or even cut short, the first time a union comes around. But when that union shows up again we see a different game plan. Much of the information and the inside contacts a union needs will be at hand for a later organizing effort. The process will be much shorter the second time, if it is the same union. There is apt to be cooperation between unions in this only where the information-owning union has no further designs on the employee group.

The preliminary stage, then, when there has been an earlier organizing try may be so short as to defy detection by the foremen, group leaders or anyone else not on the "inside." If there is no substantial sub rosa stage, all of the foregoing elements of short range campaigning, except fence-mending, must be fitted in quickly by company campaign management.

Other factors will come into play for the open phase of campaigning, when a union begins to advertise publicly or announces to the company its presence or perhaps demands recognition or sends a petition to the NLRB for an election.

The Open Campaign Phase

The counter campaign moves with more urgency when the union campaign becomes known and more precisely, when the union first knows that its campaign is known. To this point the organizing effort may have seemed to ebb and flow, with active periods and inactive periods. Now it is likely the activity will continue and will grow. A new set of actions must be taken by the company.

The company's options begin to narrow when the union presence is public knowledge. The NLRB has held that when an employer is told, ". . . some of us have signed authorization cards," he is on notice that the union is active and can no longer offer and give improvements in wages, hours and work conditions. His acts may be ruled unfair labor practices. So after this point, communications and other routine personnel actions must be weighed for the possible charge of unfair labor practice.

Open Campaign—Before NLRB Hearing

It is not possible to schedule activities for the open campaigning when no election has been requested and no NLRB hearing has been held. The base period is unknown, as in the sub rosa stage. But important preparations must be made in the areas of training, obtaining legal counsel and preparing for forthcoming strategy decisions.

Training
Supervisors and security people will be given all the facts known about the union. The company's campaign plan will be described in general. The legal requirements will be clarified. Supervisors must be cautioned that, if discipline is to be imposed upon an employee it must not be linked with union activity in any comment to workers.

Legal Counsel
When a demand for recognition arrives, the first step is a check of the demand itself by legal counsel. The employer is obliged to respond in some way if there is a clear claim that the union has a majority, a clear description of a legal bargaining unit and a clear request for bargaining.

Also, counsel should be alerted to prepare for moving to end an illegal strike, if that threat is present. The proper police officials should be warned in advance if there is any chance of law violation by the union's men.

Campaign Strategy

The union's demand, if it is in proper form, presents the campaign manager with alternatives: a) express doubt of the majority and suggest to the union that it get an election through the NLRB (this is the most common response to a demand) b) send an "employer petition" for an election to the Board. A move that is especially effective when the feedback indicates the union is still weak. A decisive defeat will discourage further attempts by this, and other, unions. It is also the response that will steer clear of any danger of being accused of refusing to bargain. A disadvantage of the employer petition idea is that the union may make much of the employer's asking for an election, implying the company has no objection to a union.

A third, seldom advisable, course is to suggest a privately held election among the employees or agree to one if the union has asked for it. This would produce a fast settlement, which may at times be to the employer's advantage. But if the union has asked for such an election, one must assume the union is ready.

A union or employer petition to the NLRB brings further restrictions to the employer's campaign. This is the start of the "pre-election period" in which the NLRB may set aside the results of an election, because of conduct by the employer or union that interferes with the election. The Board requires a "laboratory atmosphere" for its elections. Company actions and communications which do not amount to unfair labor practices may yet interfere with the Board's election process. The penalty for doing this is a rerun of the election, if the union loses.

When a petition has gone to the Board, the possibility of a "consent election" agreement presents another key strategy decision to the company. Within a week or two after the Board receives a petition a representative will hold a conference of the union, the company and, possibly, employees. Attendance is voluntary. He will try to arrange an election by getting agreement on such items as a) coverage by the National Labor Management Relations Act, b) a list of the eligible voters, c) makeup of the bargaining unit and d) the place and time of the election. This brings an early election which may not be favorable, but it gives the employer some ability to shape the bargaining unit and to have the election at a convenient time in return for consenting to the election.

In order to get an election, via the consent route, without the time and expense of a hearing, unions often make concessions on the key points: the eligibility of voters and the groups to be included in the bargaining unit. The NLRB will usually permit three to four weeks to prepare a campaign in return for not having to hold a hearing.

Disagreements about eligibility arise when there is doubt whether a particular employee is a "supervisor" according to the law; whether "fringe" employees, such as timekeepers, plant clerical people and the like are properly part of the unit; whether people laid off or dismissed should be allowed to vote; etc. The employer or union may be able to count some friends in the jobs that are in dispute and the final decision becomes important.

Similarly, there are often voting advantages to be gained by having certain groups included in the voting unit. More often it is a question of combatting union gerrymandering to include groups that are solidly organized. The employer usually favors a larger, logical bargaining unit where the workers have a real community of interest and function. In the event of a loss, a coherent bargaining unit makes good business sense.

If there is no agreement between the parties, a hearing will be scheduled. This will certainly consume more time and if an issue is raised that will call for a decision by the Board in Washington (a regional office of the Board will have handled it to this point) a long delay will ensue.

To give an idea of the timing involved: a petition to the Board, when one of the parties will not enter into a consent election, will be followed by a hearing within about 21 days. A full hearing may last the better part of a week. About five days are needed to print the record (plus an additional seven days or so if briefs are filed at the conclusion of the hearing) and then another two to three weeks for a decision to be handed down on the points in dispute. About 21 days' notice will then be given of the election date.

Open Campaign—Before Election Date is Firm

Presuming a hearing has been held, there will be a period of three to four weeks before a date is set for the election. The employer's final campaign must be readied in this time. Specific acts at specific times should be planned with the purpose of giving each worker who will vote complete information on the question of unionism by the time he steps into the voting booth.

A type of scheduling can be done for this in-between period:

Hearing Plus 1 Day: Prepare a letter informing the employees of the developments in the hearing and of what may be expected of the NLRB and what the union might say and do. Hold meeting of supervisors and managers to preview the letter and to answer questions.

Hearing Plus 2 Days: Mail letter to employees' homes.

As time is available, prepare final campaign plan.

Daily meeting of campaign leadership to assess news and pass on communications to employees.

Daily or more frequent posting of "Truth Forum" notices on boards, responding to union statements or claims.

Weekly "checkout" of supervisors.

A regular "checkout" of each supervisor of people in the voting unit is a recommended feature of many short range plans. In this technique the boss will be asked to classify each of his people as pro-union, pro-company, or undecided and he will be asked about people under others' supervision, if he has any information on which to form an opinion. He will also be quizzed on the individual quirks and interests of his people, and such other items as each one's "calling" name, the name of the wife, how many children and the like. This line of questioning is mostly for the purpose of addressing communications and getting a profile of the audience for communications, to bring emphasis on the right subjects, but clearly some of it is to learn how much the supervisor knows about his people and to lead him to take more personal interest in them, if this would help.

The campaign leadership has decisions to make and actions to take in the areas of communication, campaign "tone" and campaign content. All the while the union may be quite active, even though the date of the election is not yet known. It is a busy time.

Communicating

The major burden of the plan for short range action is communicating. A communication plan for this campaign consists, first, of a systematic way to gather and handle information on the union organizers' moves, on employee activity both for and against the union, on the union's campaign approach and on the progress of the campaign among the employees. All such information must be funneled to the company's campaign leadership for evaluation. Sources of campaign information must be kept open, taking care however, that employees are not questioned and that spying does not occur. The big decisions about the content and tone of the company's campaign rely on this upward flow of information.

Communication downward is next in the plan. This starts with setting up a net by which news and instructions can be passed rapidly to the supervision. Multiple methods are best. Meetings, a daily newsletter or a recorded telephone message can be used for this.

Next come the methods for communicating with employees. A company's early short range communication planning will be more concerned with the methods to be used in communication than with subject matter. Certain subjects will be universally useful to the company in the defense against unionism—the disadvantages of unionism for the employees, the company's strong points and messages along these lines may be blocked out in advance. But the more important communications are those that are in response to the situation: particulars about the union's leadership and activity elsewhere, answers to false and misleading union claims, current wage and benefit comparisons, the out-of-pocket cost of being a member of the union, unsavory clauses from the union's contracts with other employers (such as "super-seniority" for local officials of the union or the requirement that an employee must belong to the union to keep his job). These cannot be prepared long in advance.

One thinks immediately of a letter to the employee's home when he thinks of company communication. The letter to the home is only one of many channels available. It is also the best channel for those matters that involve the man's entire family: matters such as job security, pay, medical benefits and the like. However, the samples used later are only to suggest content, not to imply that a letter or other writing is the preferred way. Along with letters and various mailings to the employees' homes (mailings which might include reports of stockholder meetings, annual reports, quarterly financial reports and perhaps a company magazine) bulletin boards, reading racks, handbills, poster displays, recorded telephone messages, closed circuit TV, intercom systems, pay check envelope stuffers, billboards and radio-TV-newspaper advertising can be pressed into service.

One company's messages were unusual but the NLRB Regional Director had no hesitation in giving them an OK, in answer to the losing union's protest. Some of them were:
The things you get with a union—dues, fines and assessments.
Man who votes YES puts his destiny in another man's hands.
No Union: No Fines—No Assessments—No Dues—No Strikes.
Man who does not find time to vote may find time to pay union dues.
Employees' words speak louder to company than voice of outsider.
The Regional Director also okayed the way these thoughts were conveyed: Fortune Cookies!

But leading all the media is face-to-face communication: every day between the supervisor and his people; regularly, in visits by higher management to the workplace; periodically, in talks at company-sponsored picnics, dinners, barbecues and social events large and small; and one time, a large group "captive audience" address as the campaign nears an end.

It is the duty of the leadership, or the appointed communication man, to decide which channel shall convey each subject and to see that all necessary arrangements are made to deliver the message. In the case of face-to-face talks by the immediate supervisor, subject matter may be outlined daily for him along with suggestions on how to pass it on.

Company Campaign Tone

Campaign headquarters must determine the company's campaign style and tone, making the decision first of all, whether to be extra cautious to remain pure, (to be certain that the election will not be set aside or an unfair labor practice found that would undercut what could have been an easy victory) or to risk having the election rerun by going all out in the campaigning. The company must not appear neutral. Too shrill a voice may hurt the company's image, but on the other hand too much dignity can lose the election. The company must not be too proud to fight.

Campaign Content

What will the company's overall message be? The leadership may judge that the best chance lies in spotlighting the good things about the company rather than the bad about the union, or build the company image by identifying with and building around people in management who are popular and well accepted by the men. Always the final purpose is to move the men to think, and vote NO UNION on election day. These are the kinds of questions that confront the men handling the company counter-campaign.

Open Campaign—After Election Date Known

When the election day and time is fixed, a company campaign calendar can be drawn up which will set times for the major communication efforts, meetings and other check points. For an election three weeks away the plan for working days until the election might look like this:

15—Continue daily campaign leadership meeting

15—Continue daily "Truth Forum" postings

15—Dinner meeting with all supervision, stressing importance of information, explaining campaign organization, reviewing forthcoming letter to employees.

14—Manager's letter to employees' homes regarding issues, the urgent need to vote, and information on the date, time and place of the election.

13—Supervisor checkout.

12—Group meeting of supervisors to summarize activities and review forthcoming manager's letter.

Place posters and spot "pickup" materials to supplement "Truth Forum" postings.

11—Management letter to employees on theme of union disadvantages, timed to arrive on weekend.

9—Change posters and "pick-ups".

8—Speeches by manager or superintendents to individual work groups.

7—Supervisor checkout. Supervisor group meeting to preview letter to employees.

6—Letters to employees from their own department heads regarding issues in the individual work groups.

5—Change posters and "pick-ups".

4—Meeting of all supervisors, group checkout, final plans, instructions for last days of campaign and preview of letter.

3—Letter to employees' homes, detailing benefits gained without a union and emphasizing that signing a union card does not oblige them to vote YES. Change posters.

1—Captive audience speech—a comprehensive talk about the issues, held at the workplace on company time for all employees.

Posters, "pick-ups" updated.

Telephoned reminders to vote, offers to answer questions.

0—Election

The campaign is planned to "peak" on the eve of the election, underlining a) "getting out the vote", b) the message that employees have the secret ballot and c) that voters have no duty to vote for the union even though they have signed the union's authorization cards.

The Post-Election Period

The election itself is almost an anti-climax, but presuming the company is successful, there are important steps to be taken that are usually led by the company campaign leadership (though these steps are properly part of the long range plan between elections). They involve

1. Tapering off the communicating with employees smoothly, so it will not appear the management is no longer interested in them now that it has what it wants.

2. Attacking the problems that have been troubling the workers and that the union has spotlighted in the campaign. Company action should be taken openly and publicized, if appropriate to do so.

3. Auditing supervisor performance in campaigning as a guide to training needs and coaching during period of peace.

4. Identifying strong pro-company employees and pro-union employees, making it quite clear the company and the supervisor, personally, appreciate the pro-company man and working to improve the attitude and outlook of the union adherent.

5. Evaluating the results of both long and short range programs in the light of events and making recommendations to higher management for needed changes, such as the expected shorter "quiet" campaign on the next try because of information the union must have gathered and the known fact that the union has a list of employee names and addresses. Some union organizers do not expect to win a major election on the first try; they call themselves "second time winners."

Conclusion

This description of the company's preparation to fend off union advances may seem long and over complicated. A small plant or office would not have so many things to do. But the fact is that preparations can be even more complex if there are special problems, such as a tense race relations picture or the presence of more than one union campaigning. Companies have successfully stayed union-free without a formal plan, but nearly always the elements of a plan are present, if only in the experience and knowledge of at least one member of management.

Central Figure

Running through all these plans and actions of the company is a common thread: the key importance of the immediate supervisor of the people who are being wooed by the union. He, almost alone, provides the feedback of information on employee complaints, grievances and discomforts. He provides early warning of a union's presence on the scene. He provides feedback on the progress of the union's campaign and the company's. He provides feedback on employee attitudes and feelings. Key decisions are based on his observations. Above all, in his face-to-face communication with his people, his is the one most powerful voice at the company's disposal.

Chapter 5

White Collars & Union-Free Pockets

The supervisor of white collar people will read in his newspaper that labor leaders predict sweeping victories in the organizing battle for the white collar and that unions in convention are setting ambitious goals in white collar membership. He will read a press release from the NLRB pointing out that unions are winning 55% of elections in white collar units. He will attend a management seminar and be told by a dean of a college of business that unionization of white collar people will surely take a great leap forward in the next few years.

The supervisor may look about and find that within his own company his group of white collar people is really a "pocket" in an otherwise solidly unionized location. It is easy to understand that he will wonder why his people are still union-free and will doubt his and his company's ability to defend against an organizing attempt.

Union Label for the White Collar?

The union-free white collar supervisor need not feel helpless at the approach of a union. The union leadership and the scholars have found their crystal balls cloudy. As the unions win 50-55% of elections they take in at most 10,000 new members (presuming that every voter later joins the union), an almost negligible percentage of the nearly 25 million organizable white collar people in the work force.

The unions' own data on membership, showing many more new members than the NLRB election results, only add up to maintaining a level percentage of the white collar work force, ten to twelve percent, over many years. The unions' figures may be presumed accurate or even conservative, since unions belonging to the AFL-CIO pay per capita tax on any member reported. This tends to minimize reported membership totals. The NLRB election is only one route to union membership. Accessions to the union ranks also come from employers' recognizing a union without an election; federal, state and municipal employees entering into a bargaining relationship by the appropriate channel, *not* through the NLRB; and private sector employees coming in through State Board election procedures, by privately held elections or card checks.

The figures do not even mean that a company's chances are less than 50% at the time a union begins to organize. It has been pointed out earlier that the Board's statistics include many unopposed elections; that there is careful selection by the union with the result that only the best prospects for a victory are brought under the union guns; that there is another selection process before a petition is filed; and finally that about a third of all petitions filed are withdrawn or dismissed.

So the odds, when the company is prepared to resist, are actually very good. Another factor favoring the company is the splintered attack by the union movement as a whole. All the major unions are in the white collar business. The two leading organizers of white collar people are the Teamsters and the Electrical Workers. For the unions this seems a natural thing to do, but the man working as an artist in an advertising agency may wonder what kind of representation the Mine Workers can give him.

Akin to this fragmented approach is the idea that the unions do not really have a good handle on the problem. Perhaps there is none to be had. But in any event many unions insist on the same approach to blue and white alike; a meat-on-the-table, down-with-the-company theme. Others think a very special approach is called for. But there is yet no password or rallying cry and the unions can't get off the ground.

The Genus White Collar

The unions who take a different approach to the white collar workers are probably on the right track. The experienced supervisor knows that, labor-relations-wise, the white collar is a breed apart. Some of the unions' trouble may be traced to too much generalizing about "the white collar." The "white collar" is a clerical worker, a retail sales clerk, an engineer working at the drawing board, a computer operator or service man, a bookkeeper or clerk, a laboratory technician and many other things. Much of the following is also generalizing, but it is done to bring out the key differences between blue collar workers and a few samples of the large array of workers included in the term "white collar."

The samples chosen study typical white collars with quite different jobs, work conditions, background and skills. There is no intent to suggest that these make up the white collar universe. Each supervisor must judge whether any worker, workplace or problem taken up here fits his own pistol before acting on any advice he finds here.

Four main white collar groups can be isolated: professionals, clericals, technicians and sales people.

Professionals

The differences between the professional employee and other workers were known to Congress when it forbade the NLRB to declare "appropriate" any bargaining unit which includes both professionals and non-professionals unless a majority of the professionals vote for inclusion in such unit.

A professional is defined by the NLRB as "any employee engaged in work a) predominantly intellectual in character as opposed to routine mental, mechanical or physical work, b) involving the consistent exercise of discretion and judgment in its performance, c) of such a character that the output produced or the results accomplished cannot be standardized in relationship to a given period of time, and d) requiring knowledge of an advanced type in a field of science or learning customarily acquired by a prolonged course of specialized intellectual instruction. . ."

If he is a supervisor, the engineer is not covered by the Act at all, but he must *supervise.* Two examples of engineers included in bargaining units are: a) those who laid out the day-to-day work of crews who were not responsible to them; and b) engineers who could ask lower-ranked engineers for assistance, but had only technical guidance of their efforts.

Exempt status under the Fair Labor Standards Act does not dictate NLRB coverage.

The work performed, not the employee's education, is the yardstick. Examples of employees ruled *not* professionals are: accountants, time study engineers, routine lab analysts and editorial employees of a newspaper.

The professional group creates problems for a union beyond the technicalities raised by the NLRB. Organizers run into many obstacles:

1. Professionals tend to identify with management and unions find it difficult to make them see the company as "the enemy".

2. In the same vein, many professionals oppose unionism on principle, feeling that unions have brought blue collar workers to a sorry state of mediocrity.

3. Professionals, particularly engineers, expect to "climb the ladder". Unions have always had their best success where workers feel they have reached their limit. Generally, the best leaders and the strongest motivated, who otherwise might have been the nucleus of union leadership *have* climbed the ladder and have been promoted to management and are no longer available to the union.

4. Engineering and professional unions are less effective. They strike, but the work goes on as management people do the necessary professional work.

5. The professional does not believe a union can give him status, certainly not that kind that is freely given by the management and not that kind that will elevate him relative to his peers.

6. Professionals tend to rely on "motivators", things such as achievement, recognition, responsibility, growth-advancement and meaningful satisfying work in itself. These are not the unions' stock in trade.

Quasi-Unions

A final frustration for the old-line union organizer is the variety of union-like groups competing for the professional's dues dollar:

Professional Societies have some interest in conditions of work, but are fundamentally standards setting, possibly accreditation groups. The American Institute of Chemical Engineers is an example of this kind of group.

Professional Associations are strongly concerned with pay and other job matters. They may be national in scope, like the National Society of Professional Engineers, or they may be a group within one company or at a single company location. This sort of group may collect pay data from sources both inside and outside the company and distribute it to members; perhaps they will discuss job matters with the company, but they will not bargain or enter into labor contracts.

One-Company Unions or Associations are groups that will be usually certified by the NLRB and will bargain about work condition. They may be associated with a professional union, such as the Marine Engineers Beneficial Association. Typically, there is no formal hookup with blue collar groups in the same company or locality.

Professional-Technical Affiliates of Established Unions whose members are mostly blue collar workers. Such an affiliate may operate as a department of the mother union and exercise independent power and often will have a professional-sounding name.

Primarily Professional Unions operating on a multi-company basis. These usually do business under their own name, like the Marine Engineers, but may have smaller one-company or one-area organizations in the fold.

Clericals

From the standpoint of the union organizer the chief differences between clerical and blue collar workers are found in the workers themselves, in the employee-management relationship and in the work setting.

Clericals as a group have a relatively large number of females. Surveys indicate that the ladies value elements such as fairness, appreciation of work, and pleasant "social" relations on the job and are repulsed by the threat of strikes and violence that a union implies. Many of them are not the head of a family, but are single or are supplementing a family income and do not have a basic dependency on the job. They do not feel the pressure that the head of a family feels. When dissatisfied they are more likely to seek a new job than attempt to improve the pay and conditions of the one they have by action against the company. These needs point toward maintaining a good relationship with the supervision and the higher management. True, in this kind of work setting there will be those who would prefer strict seniority for moving up the ladder and there will be young, liberal, activist, "lightly" college-trained people who are disposed to welcome a union, but on the whole it is a bad scene for the organizer.

The relationships between employee and supervisor and employee and manager are perhaps the most striking difference between white collar clerical and blue collar people.

The clerical worker is much more likely to see the manager in a more favorable light, on his own ground, at ease and acquainted on a first name basis, in many cases. In contrast, at the plant the manager is apt to be hustled through by supervisors and allowed to slow down only at places where the reception will be good. He may not visit often enough to associate faces and names. This situation has a strong negative effect, as when he must be introduced to the same people repeatedly, over a period of years.

The work of the clerical tends to be in the nature of helping the supervisor in his duties, rather than to be turning out the product, under supervision. His work goals, then, tend to become those of his supervisor and his supervisor's success is his success. In this way many white collar people find their personal work goals and company goals very nearly the same.

The work setting is better. Clericals, like other white collar people, will usually have much more pleasant, quieter, cleaner work areas and better eating and sanitary facilities than the average blue collar worker. Organizers can rarely build up an issue on these grounds. Additionally, there is apt to be greater fellowship between people of various departments and a more active social life at work. The supervisor will usually be a part of the work's social life, making for much easier communication on non-work matters including, especially, subjects such as union activity among the employees.

The group is much more likely to be mixed, male and female, than the ordinary blue collar group. This creates a more mannered, polite setting. The clerical worker may work in a public building occupied by many other companies rather than on company-owned plant property; may car-pool with clerical employees of other companies who have the same starting time.

The equipment operated by the clerical will require more brain and less brawn than that of the typical blue collar. The pay of the clerical worker, again like other white collars, will usually be by the calendar rather than by the clock. The salaried status often carries with it more liberal benefits in sick pay, medical, pension, leave of absence and profit sharing.

Technicals

The technician will tend to prize the layer of education and training that sets him apart from the blue collar worker. He will seek in his work the responsibility and status of the professionals working about him. Being in a union group would tend to set him apart from them, and farther below the professionals he envies.

The technician group is commonly assumed to be the group that will grow wildly in the future. Experts opine that in the truly automated plant the dividing line between blue collar and technicals will be blurred in the future as production work becomes more and more like the technician's job. These new "light blue" collar jobs are expected to be occupied from the top, from the white collar technicians, rather than from below.

While sharing pleasant working conditions and the "calendar" pay and more liberal benefits enjoyed by the clericals, most technicals feel themselves set apart by the higher standards of their calling. They want the status of the professional. The company cannot give this in many cases, but the union can never give it. Unionization means to him that he will be brought down to the level of the blue collar working stiff.

Sales People

Sales jobs are so far removed from the average blue collar it is not practical to point to any one or two elements as key differences. The person-to-person skills and techniques involved in sales work have no application to most blue collar jobs. However, the unions have made headway in some areas of sales work.

Within the sales field, there is a vast gulf between the work life of a field "technical service man" (where unionism is rarely found) and a retail sales clerk in a large department store, where unions have organized many units. The sales workers who seldom choose unions differ from the more union prone sales people in matters such as pay (higher pay and pay on a commission basis directly related to performance); freedom to choose their own approach in selling; to plan their own day and to move about. Interestingly, research has indicated that mobility, even within the confines of a plant, is a factor contributing to higher morale and better productivity.

Retail clerks have proved more inclined to accept unions than their outside colleagues or clerical workers and technicians. It is thought this is because of a) the more distant relationship between worker and supervisor—the sales worker is the one putting forth the productive effort, under supervision, rather than helping a supervisor to reach his goals; b) the pay is often inferior; c) the working conditions are not usually favorable and d) the work is not so satisfying as that of the average clerical or technician job.

In any event, here is good proof that a white collar, of itself, does not confer immunity from unionism on the wearer.

A supervisor will usually have only one and seldom more than two of these types of white collar workers to manage. These remarks about each are not to suggest that there is a single key for his group; they are only to point out the great diversity of the "white collar" and the enormity of the problem faced by the unions in organizing white collar workers. The supervisor may find these factors and feelings alive in his group, but the questions are still person by person and the answers are still person *to* person.

What Company and Supervisor Do—Long Range

Employers of white collar people need not follow blindly the long range plans prescribed for the average blue collar union-free group. Since action of an employer depends heavily on the union climate in the area, general advice is not practical. That climate may range from a state of near total inactivity to one in which organizing campaigns are underway at other companies and the white collar group is an island in the midst of unionized people. In this light, correct employer action may range from routine conduct of good employee relations to determined, urgent, long-run defensive planning and follow-through.

In most areas the unionized white collar group is the exception and a low level of union organizing activity most often prevails. The long range plan is much the same in a white collar group as in any group. It is first a searching self-audit on a coldly factual basis. Strengths and weaknesses are evaluated. Goals and action plans are built, to correct failings and build on strengths. Priorities are set and actions taken.

In the audit, the factors that usually need attention are the business environment, the unions, the employee, the work environment, the specific preparations, the pay-benefits-practices situation and training-communication.

The Business Environment

The factors in the business setting that are often important in a long range defense plan count for little where the white collar group is concerned. The local labor market declines in importance as many of the white collar group are "imports", and many of the white collar jobs are not so sensitive to supply and demand because the skills needed are usually not narrow as in the case of craftsmen. The attitude of law enforcement people is seldom worth worry, since white collar organizing is rarely marked by violence or law-breaking (action such as this on the part of a union may have an unfavorable backlash). It is rare, too, that a white collar group will be of such a size that community racial or ethnic problems can be greatly affected by employer action.

The Union

The union most likely to appear is more easily identified in a white collar group than in most blue collar situations. The question is whether to do anything about it. When the white collars are a "pocket" in the midst of many unionized people the potential organizing union is well known, it is the "inside" union. This situation, where a group is a pocket of non-union people, calls for special treatment. It will be discussed separately, since the "pocket" is not always white collar.

The important question is whether the incumbent unions in the near vicinity or within the same company stress the signing of white collar people. If so, how do they usually go about it? If there is no union close at hand the gathering of information on the white collar oriented unions can wait until there is evidence that a particular union is becoming active in the local scene.

The Employee

Study of the employee group and of the individual employee is just as important in the long range defense in white as it is in blue collar work groups. Do they identify with the company? Is their morale high? Have the informal leaders been identified? Are complainers, loafers and mediocrities given thoughtful attention?

The Work Environment

Again, the total work setting is vital in the long range and a subject of rigid self-appraisal. We have seen that more pleasant working conditions are advanced as one of the prime reasons for the failure of unions to sweep the white collar field. Besides the physical comforts, is an effort made to create fulfilling, complete jobs?

The Specific Preparations

Most of the specific actions recommended for blue collar groups apply with equal force: a solicitation rule must be established and enforced; short-range resistance plans must be kept up-to-date; legal counsel must be arranged; a policy and practices handbook (or manual, or bulletin board posting) should be at hand to clarify benefits, rules and responsibilities; and the physical layout should be arranged, if possible, to give minimum exposure to the face-to-face approach of union organizers.

Pay, Benefits and Work Practices

The name of the game does not change with white collars in the area of pay and benefits. These must meet the expectations of the employees. Any less may cause serious disaffection; any more may be largely wasted.

Most white collars, including those not exempt from the Fair Labor Standards Act, are paid on some calendar basis, usually monthly, rather than strictly by the hour. This practice is often cited by the organizers as a stumbling block. Practices of this sort, that tend to promote the status and the unique quality of the white collar person, should be sought out and made part of the company "package." Examples of these are liberal sick pay plans, less restrictive leave of absence policies, easier permission to take time off during the work day and similar policies.

Training-Communication

Most of the thrust of the long range communications program in the large blue collar group is toward setting up or improving information channels and building company credibility. These are not usually great problems in a white collar group, but if needed, communication improvement should be given highest priority.

The supervisor of white collar people has a special duty to keep his person-to-person communicating skills sharp: in white collar organizing there is often no exploratory campaign and, frequently, no open card-soliciting drive, so early warning of a union approach assumes highest importance. The supervisor is the key man in upward communication flow and he must master the techniques that will give warning from below. If even the smallest hint is heard of union activity, he must report it quickly and the management must follow through with a thorough check.

Should training be carried to the work group? A fundamental in the long range defense is informing employees, not just managers and foremen, of the company's feeling about unionism. This is done both in orientation of new employees and on an ongoing basis, before there is any union threat. It is good advice where there is a real question. It presumes that the group of workers will be approached by unions, other groups like them have unions, and that the members of the group know these facts. It may *not* be good advice for a white collar group, however. Here, a union group is the exception and the chance of an organizing drive may be slight. The company might seem hysterical, proclaiming its distaste for unions when the thought of unionizing was far from the minds of the employees. It may have the effect of creating an interest.

Each case is different, and where the group is a "pocket" of union-free people, especially, employees should know the company's attitude. In most white collar groups a formal program to tell employees of the company's stand on unionism is not recommended.

What Company and Supervisor Do, Short Range

What and how much to do becomes a key decision when there is an unconfirmed belief that a union is at work among the white collars. A good supervisor or manager has the good sense to let well enough alone. Overaction is not only wasteful of effort and resources, but may actually pique curiosity about unionism among employees. But where there is a fair reason to believe a union is eying his group, the wise manager favors the action route, because to him what seems to be a low level of union activity may actually be poor upward communication.

A company's technique for short range resistance is influenced heavily by differences in the approach of the union, in the environment and in the white collar worker themselves. The union's campaign will be conducted in a much quieter way, usually, than in plant organizing. Face to face contacts at home and on the job are featured and written campaign materials are heavily used, reflecting the higher educational level of the white collar people.

The Union Message

The content of the union's message may be different. The union will not omit the bread and butter issues, but will also promise greater participation in the formation of the management's personnel policies and even in business policies. Participation in decisions becomes more important as one moves up the white collar ladder to the teachers and professionals. The union will say, "Have a vote in your future!"

The union will appeal to some of the higher moral and social virtues: "Perhaps you, personally, don't need a union; you are a man of high skill and can get a job anywhere, but how about the others working here? They need the help that your prestige and leadership can offer."

The many female white collar workers will be promised deliverance from the attitude that they are temporarily on the work scene and in the long run only seek homemaking careers. The inequities that often grow between skilled clerical workers and the totally unskilled plant workers who are better paid are trotted out and viewed from all angles.

Employees are promised the security and clarity of a union contract signed by the company and especially where the company has fallen into favoritism practices, the security and regularity of advancement that a seniority system offers.

Union methods of communication will be adapted to the situation. Clerical units tend to be smaller, often located in public buildings, and the workers will be more sophisticated. This means we will seldom see the sound trucks, the billboards and the newspaper advertising. We may see handbilling, more written content than cartoons and we will see much more reliance on the inside organizing cadre. White collar workers normally are able to move about and there is wider acquaintanceship between various sections and departments. The word can travel quickly and covertly.

The Employer Short Range Campaign

With this kind of approach it is clear the supervisor and manager will have a challenge on their hands when an open union campaign with a set election date lies ahead. When the voting date is known, a schedule should be prepared much like the one used in the normal campaign. Two important variations may be necessary. In the usual white collar organizing campaign the pattern of charges and countercharges may not emerge; this eliminates the need for quick bulletin board "Truth Forum" or "Truth Digest" notices. Second, there can be added to the schedule such events as dinners, theater parties and the like for husband and wife with workers, supervisors and managers invited. Here the propagandizing should not be heavy. The detailed issues should be saved for a captive audience meeting of workers only, although the meeting may be referred to, or even promised, at the social gathering.

Supervisor meetings and supervisor checkouts are important in the white collar location. The white collar organizer will be depending heavily on his in-office organizers. Supervisors must remember to take no discriminatory action against employees for union activities. They must be constantly alert for trends in employee attitudes and loyalties in a campaign of this sort, because the intensity and progress of the campaign is not as easy to gauge as when there is handbilling and union meetings going on. It is all the more important to identify the informal leaders of the employee group, since the social structure is more strongly set and is wider in scope due to the mobility they enjoy. If there is a pro-union feeling, it is more apt to extend over the entire unit than to be confined to a few sections.

The employer campaign is quieter in tone, but the management must never fall into the error of relying on the pro-management orientation of the employees. Even when pro-management attitudes are strong, a clever organizer can pitch his appeal so that the company is not attacked and employees are led to feel that a vote for the union is not necessarily a vote against the management. A dual allegiance is cultivated. Aloofness is as sure a loser in the white collar campaign as it is in a blue collar one.

Some managers feel that overreaction only draws attention to the union movement and dignifies it. There is truth in this and overreaction is never wise. The extent of company action is a matter for judgment, but the great error still lies in failing to react at all.

The content of the employer's message in the short run defense is keyed to the situation and the type of employee. The employer must first of all have an accurate reading on the union's choice of issues and must be careful to set straight non-truths and half-truths. Affirmatively, the employer can usually emphasize the main factors that lead white collar units to remain non-union in the first place:

1. Threat of a breakdown of congenial friendly relations between worker and manager, worker and supervisor and worker and worker.

2. Tendency of unionism to lead to mediocrity, with advancement based on factors other than demonstrated ability.

3. The tendency of unionism to submerge individuality.

4. The threat that white collar groups will be called out on strike to help other workers of the same union, perhaps in other companies.

5. The closer identification with the work goals of the supervisor.

6. The more desirable work place, practices, status and benefits.

The supervisor and the manger must not underestimate the power of their actions in the campaign of defense against unionism. The workers' closer ties to the company and closer association with supervisor and manager make him not only disposed to vote down the union, but also make him more disposed to accept and act on information from company sources. Union white collar organizers time and again mention the company's counter-campaign as a reason for defeat.

What to do where you perceive you can win against a union drive without effort? This is the kind of problem it is a pleasure to have. It is a judgment call, but most times wage a strong campaign anyway because: a) the union may be hiding its strength; b) the union may be forced to withdraw its petition for election; c) a crushing defeat is a powerful deterrent to any union trying again later; d) a decisive victory gives your people a feeling that they have overcome an outside threat; and e) the campaign can stress the credibility and fair dealing of the company, rather than unsavory aspects of the union, making for an easier defense next time.

Pockets of Union-Free People

The manager and supervisor faced with a situation in which the non-union group is a pocket, an island, in a largely unionized workplace are working against greater odds. Though the white collar group often is a "pocket", the "pocket" is a distinct problem. It may be a few blue collars that were not included in the original bargaining unit for one reason or another.

One study of a large number of white collar elections has found unions winning in 55% of the votes where a union already on the scene was on the ballot; winning an even 50% where there was a union on the scene other than the union on the ballot; and winning only 32% where no union was already on the scene. The employer's chances are far worse when a union has a foothold.

It must come as no surprise that the two leading organizers of white collar people are the Teamsters and the Electrical Workers, not any of the unions specializing in the white collar field. Clearly, these two are picking off the white collar in locations where they represent the other workers.

The study might suggest that the company with no union has been managing its dealings with its people better, to bring about its union-free condition. But even if the partially unionized company manages well, there are cogent reasons why the union's chances of success are better when a union is entrenched.

1. The union on the scene has a great edge in information. In the long run game, it needs no special effort to pick up all the vital facts and the names of potential leaders in the unorganized groups. In the actual campaign, news of minor upsets in good relations is easily had and cases of dissatisfaction, hurt feelings and insecurity are common knowledge.

Other unions may have access to this information from the "inside" union if it is not interested in the pocket or when the work is not in the union's jurisdiction.

2. The union on the scene can play a waiting game and make its move only when the wind is right. The negative side of this idea may suggest that the big statistical edge is an illusion: the union is much better informed on when the wind is *not* right and does not risk an election which it has no good chance to win.

3. The union on the scene presents a powerful threat of an organizing strike. To a lesser degree, an incumbent union may honor another

union's picket line in an organizing strike. If barred from striking by its contract, a union can generate "job action"—foot dragging, refusing to work overtime, doing sloppy work, filing nuisance grievances—to bring pressure on the employer.

4. An inside union may bring pressure in contract negotiations to include the unorganized people in its bargaining unit by a) voluntary recognition by the employer, or b) agreement by the employer to maintain a fatal "neutral" posture in an election.

Company Action

Taking a clear view of the situation, the manager will react differently to the two situations, where the union most likely to be a threat is the "inside" union and where it is some other union.

When the threatening union is the one in the plant, the situation may be very delicate. The company is vulnerable because of the union's information edge, its ability to play the waiting game, the possibility it will bring pressure in negotiations and the strike threat.

When the threatening union is "outside," the company finds itself in a setting more nearly like the no-union one: the union has no information advantage except as individual unionists pass the word because of their support of the union movement in general; and the union cannot wait, if it drags out the organizing drive, it becomes too expensive. However, the company will still be vulnerable to organizing strikes if the "in" union honors the picket lines as expected.

If the unionized group is the island and has a minority of the work force, there is no special strike threat. Such a union does have the advantage of accurate and up-to-date information and plenty of time to wait for a promising moment.

Defending the Pocket—Long Range Plan

The manager and supervisor must not boggle at the high odds. The odds may not, in fact, be so high since something has made this group stay union-free to this moment, so it will likely not be a pushover for the first organizer who comes along. A number of points should be noted in the long range defense of the "pocket":

1. The company should identify the factors that have led the group to stay union-free and build on them.

2. It is usually easy to identify the probable union threat, where the "in" union is interested in the union-free people. In this instance it is

not necessary to gather background information on the union. In any event there is little use for it. If the probable organizer is an outside union, the same kind of information about it should be secured as in the normal long range defense.

3. Pay, fringes and all working conditions must be kept at levels at least comparable to similar work in the union group. There is no need here to seek out the area norms or spend a lot of time divining the expectations of the union-free people, simply be certain these items can be favorably compared to those of the union group.

This is best done by withholding major adjustments until after union negotiations are completed. Many managers rebel at the idea, thinking the non-union people will give the union credit for anything bestowed on them. They will feel like "free riders". This is a valid point. The alternative, though, is to adjust the non-union people first, which adjustment then becomes the "floor" from which the union will commence bargaining. Any concession won beyond it forces the management, to maintain equality of treatment, to return later and give the concession to the non-union group. This feeds the "free-rider" syndrome even more strongly, and produces much more expensive settlements.

Actually, it has never been shown that waiting until after a union settlement to "settle" with the union-free people has any tendency to drive them into the arms of the union. They can appreciate the problem of the company and they may even root for the union to get a good bargain, but they can also see that their own position is very good indeed.

Many companies, when there is a clear-cut settlement covering all their union people, make it a practice to give a slightly sweeter package to the union-free group. There might be, for example, a more liberal sickness benefits plan or one administered in a more trusting way. Not requiring irksome physicians' reports to establish proof of disability, for example. This is scarcely possible under a union contract where the slightest discipline for abuse of a plan will be challenged by grievances and arbitration.

It may also be advisable to adjust pay on something other than a one-time across-the-board basis. White collars, usually paid by the month, may have a pay review at an interval that is, perhaps, tied to the individual's employment date. The "merit" increase given under such a system should not, except in unusual cases, be less than the union's across-the-board figure in a given year.

4. Great care must be given to the handling of situations such as equipment changes, job duty changes, layoffs and discipline that can

cause employee unrest. This can be picked up quickly by the union and acted upon.

5. Physical and organizational arrangements become important in discouraging the spread of unionism. Throwing union-free people into contact with unionized people is clearly not a good idea. But there are also many actions that can be taken to impede what contacts exist.

a. Re-locating entrances.

b. Installing different starting schedules to avoid contact at starting and quitting times. The objection may be raised that car pools will be broken up, inconveniencing employees. This is regrettable, but dissolving mixed union and non-union car pools may well cut off the single most intimate contact between members of the two groups.

c. Re-studying recreation programs that throw all groups together. All-company family affairs like a picnic or a Christmas party for the children are not likely to have any unwanted results. Many companies, though, undertake programs and put on events that accomplish little, morale-wise, and seem to have as their object making workers become better acquainted with one another—examples are intra-company athletic programs, excursions and purchase of blocks of tickets at sporting events. Where these programs bring together union and non-union people their value should be carefully weighed.

d. The work of the union-free group can often be located or re-located in a separate part of a building, in a separate building or even at a separate address.

e. Separate lunch and snack facilities or separate hours for the use of common facilities, should be provided if feasible.

The purpose of this kind of action is to cool down communication between union and non-union groups, chiefly to deny the union information it can use. In some instances it will prevent union committed employees from harassing or bringing social pressures on the non-union employees. It is not to deny the union-free people access to information: there are no magic words of persuasion that the employer need fear.

6. Planning is of high importance in defending the union-free pocket. Noting that there is usually no exploratory campaign and often no open campaign before a demand for recognition (there is often no open campaign even *after* the demand) the plan should also include a fairly complete short range campaign schedule. The long range plan should include an inquiry into the reasons the group has remained a pocket, as pointed out above. If these reasons can be spotted, long and short range plans should build around them. They may include:

a. Freedom from having to participate in a strike, particularly a strike in support of some other unionized group.

b. Enjoyment of all the benefits the unionists enjoy without paying dues and lip service to the union.

c. Having the things workers really want: advancement by ability, personal recognition, good social relationships with fellow workers and managers, varied and interesting work, etc.

Defending the Pocket—Short Range

The manager who worries himself into inaction over the possible ill feeling of his unionized people will not long have a pocket of union-free workers to enjoy. Generally, any ill feelings that occur will be on the part of the inside union's leaders, not the unionized employees generally. And if the organizing union is an outside union the inside one will often oppose it, feeling they should do any organizing that is done.

Again, planning must be sound. As noted, there may not be any time to put together a short range plan. The plan should include a schedule of campaign action covering an approximate three-week period. This schedule can be adapted from the one used in an ordinary campaign to fit the needs of the situation. The plan must also provide for courses of action in the event of an organizing strike that is supported by the union group.

The content of communications to the pocket of employees will be modified in two ways:

1. Where much of the material that is used in the ordinary campaign is informational, on unionism in general and on projection of what life at work will be like if there is a union, the people here will have an example of these before them. The communicating must start beyond this point.

2. The ideas to be communicated must take into account the performance of the union or unions on the scene. Obviously a poorly-run union provides good material, but a successful union should not be attacked directly. The employee-organizer's message may range from, "We've got a good thing here, why don't you get with us?," or "You are a bunch of free riders—you ought to have the decency to help pay for what we are getting for you!," to "If you don't come in we are going to make life miserable for you!" The company's response must be tailored to the union's approach.

The method of communicating to a pocket should be more subdued than to a normal group. While the manager should not be worried about resisting the spread of unionism, there is still nothing to be gained by flaunting his opposition before the "in" union. Oral communication, letters to the home and phone calls should be emphasized rather than bulletin boards; handouts containing material the rank and file of union people can study are to be avoided.

Affirmatively, the manager should take the lead in meeting the needs of his union-free people not only in the bread-and-butter items and in work practices, but in providing challenging work in a pleasant productive atmosphere under fair and friendly supervisors. In this respect the pocket is no different from the totally union-free plant or office: the organizers will not come around, even when they are just across the fence, when these needs are met.

Chapter 6
The Union Communicates Ideas

It has been seen that the union's final campaign for the vote of the workers may take any shape. The organizer has a number of weapons. There is no way for a supervisor to predict whether the organizer will rely chiefly on handbilling, letters to the homes, posters, or general meetings to sell his ideas. With larger groups, it may prove to be sound trucks, billboards, newspaper and radio-TV advertising. He may opt for a totally different approach and not use any of these open, mass methods; he may prefer instead to build his game plan around home visits, person-to-person contacts at the nearby coffee shop or bar or meetings of small groups or committees.

It is a good bet that the combination of these he elects to use will include a heavy salting of person-to-person communicating. Eye-opening facts about this were turned up by recent research financed by unions and conducted by San Fernando Valley State College. The college was asked to measure the impact of union organizing techniques through in-depth talks with some 500 persons, voters in NLRB elections who had been chosen as a random sample over a given period of time. They were asked what did they think influenced them or their co-workers most in the union's campaign? Three of the top four techniques named proved to be face-to-face contacts. Forty-three percent said union meetings had influenced them most. Thirty-three percent cited talks with fellow employees working for the union. Ten percent responded that discussions with union organizers in the home had been most convincing. The fourth of the top four methods, "union leaflets," named by 14%, could also be called a form of face-to-face contact; there is nearly always conversation to go along with the handout. The heading "All Others", a scattering of answers, comprises only 15% of the total. So the first four techniques assume real significance. These were the statements of all the people who had voted, both pro-union and anti-union.

The same group ranked the most important *reasons* for voting for a union. These turned out to be: a) "Collective Bargaining" and being represented by a union insures better pay and job security, b) Improved fringe benefits would result, c) The union would bring fair pay, fair promotions and seniority rights, d) There would be a grievance procedure (age seemed to bear on this reply: the old people tended to rank it higher), e) There would be control of standards of output, quotas and speedup.

The survey also found that some 25% of the anti-union voters made up their minds late in the campaign, most of these just before the election.

Emphasis on Face to Face

Supervisors can expect, then, to see unions employing more face-to-face communication. Failure here has in fact been cited by union organizing pros as one of the major reasons unions have not been able to increase their numbers importantly over the past two decades: the companies have been shooting them down at what used to be their best area of competence, the personal touch.

Here is a great message for supervisors. Despite all the advances that have been made in communicating—the fast, easy printing methods, the tape recorder, TV, canned telephone messages—the queen of the battlefield is still the infantry: the supervisor and the managers speaking face-to-face with the men.

A union-supported survey disclosed ominous news for managers of office and clerical workers. The old belief that women were not interested in union representation was challenged by a finding that women voted pro-union 14% more than men. The sample would not include a large proportion of purely clerical jobs, true, but any reliance on the fair sex, as such, to reject the union should be dismissed.

The attitudes of young people were clarified by the survey. Some had thought young people, opposed to the "establishment", would be difficult to bring to the company's viewpoint. Others had guessed the union hierarchy would itself be an "establishment" which the young would oppose. Neither was wholly right, the "young" again refusing to fit a mold. A 4% edge voted in favor of the company, not a significant figure either way. It does mean though, that the young people in the work force can be reached by the reasoned persuasion of management.

Different Strokes for Different Folks

The union campaign will not only be hard to predict as to method, it will also be flexible as to tone. What is your reaction to a statement like:

Joining our union is not an act of disloyalty to the company. It is only as disloyal as *you* make it.
And how about:
You are the kind of guy who can make his own deal or can go get a job anywhere, but how about your co-workers who are being pushed around? They need you!

Isn't this a little more persuasive to you than the wild attacks on the company you might expect of a union? It is the kind of "tone" you might find in a campaign to enlist technicians, clerical or accounting workers. You may be sure that the organizer is not going to pull any punches or adhere to any set rules to win over your people.

The unions stay alert to changes in the business climate. They respond to the trend toward the "conglomerate", as it merges many seemingly unrelated companies, by promising a "successor" clause in labor contracts to protect employees of firms involved in mergers, acquisitions or sub-contracting. This is an agreement that the contract will be observed by a "successor" company. They promise the "technological change" clause in the contract, guaranteeing retraining and continued employment for those displaced by new equipment. And for those who operate the new equipment the union will promise pay commensurate with the education, skill and ability requirements of the automated classifications. Promises are inexpensive.

The unions have taken note of the explosive increase in technicians and scientists and the fact that in the Fifties, according to one union study, production workers actually had declined in number: In all manufacturing by 9%, by 12½% in aircraft and parts, 12% in chemical and allied products and 10½% in petroleum. The organizers' message will be different. The old line unions are trying to adjust by establishing specialized departments to deal with the emerging "knowledge" workers.

Responsiveness the Key

One characteristic the supervisor can expect from union communication is that it will be effective. The grammar may not be
precise and punctuation is no object, but the message will come
across. The important fact is that the message will be coming not only
from the organizer, an outsider, but from his fellow workers, perhaps
from people he trusts and perhaps even from close personal friends.
The message will come across in a well-run union campaign.

The union also profits from an absence of responsibility. If a grave
error is made, if the law is transgressed, all the union has to lose is the
effort it has made to that time. The situation returns to the status
before the union appeared, which is no great setback for the union. So
the union can take risks. By the same token the union can delegate
authority to the man on the spot, the organizer, to make decisions and
to put out statements, releases and publications. This provides him
great flexibility and gives him the advantage of speed in composing
and cranking out the handbills and letters without need of a series of
approvals from above.

The Most-Used Themes

Let us look at some examples of union organizing themes:

How Can We?

The opening union gun may be surprisingly bland. Union campaigns are often businesslike and neutral toward employers these
days. The tone of the campaign may be deliberately low pitched or like
the canned letter in Figure 6.1, printed by a successful international
union with space for overprinting by a local union, it may be general
comment about the procedure employees can use to organize
themselves. Any kind of healthy response to a handout such as this
will bring on intensive activity. This kind of handout is also used
when a sub rosa campaign has been successful, only a few more supporters are needed and the organizer appears at the gate more to introduce himself to the workers than to communicate. In any event, if
nothing happens, there is no loss of face by the union; this was only
telling the people how to do it themselves.

What to Expect

A piece, usually in folder form, used by many unions is the warning
of what employees may expect of management in the course of an
organizing campaign. One version shows on the front cover a stylized

---

How Can We Form a Labor Union?

If you and your fellow workers want a labor union, there are several things you must do before you have a working local union set up and a contract signed with your employer.

First, a majority of the employees in your group must sign cards authorizing the union to act as your collective bargaining agent. The larger that majority is, the stronger your union will be and the better contract you can get from your boss.

After a majority of the employees have signed up with the union, the union will ask the employer to recognize it as bargaining agent for the employees and to begin contract negotiations. Sometimes the employer will agree right off to bargain with the union. More often, however, he will refuse to bargain unless and until the union is "certified" by the NLRB.

The next step is for the union to file a petition with NLRB. NLRB (a U.S. government agency) will then step in and conduct a *secret ballot* election among the employees. In this election, the employees will vote on whether or not they wish to be represented by the union.

If a majority of the employees vote in favor of the union, the NLRB will then "certify" the union. Once the union is certified, federal law requires that the employer sit down in negotiations with the union.

In all of these steps, you will need the help of a representative of _____ Union. This union will gladly send a representative to help any group which sincerely wants to organize a union.

_____ International Union, AFL-CIO

Figure 6.1. A typical canned letter used to open a union organizing campaign.

picture of a bomb, and the pamphlet is entitled, "Look Out Below." Another variation is a check list of actions to expect, with boxes to check as each occurs.

Knowing that this sort of communication may be used should convince a company of the need for doing things that should be done in the months before or between campaigns. Much of its thrust, as you will see, is that the management will become suddenly charming, generous and communicative, all because the union is on the scene. These things that are predicted can also be assumed to be those which are most damaging to the union's chances or they would not be trying to nullify the effects. Here is the "What to Expect" theme:

Look Out Below

No one is more interested in labor unions than the boss—especially when he gets wind of his employees' starting any kind of a unionizing campaign.

His interest is understandable. His actions, however, are often close to unbelievable!

He knows that his employees should be allowed to use their own judgment, BUT SOMEHOW HE DOESN'T QUITE TRUST THEIR JUDGMENT, at least to do what he wants.

He knows he'd blow his stack if the workers ever stuck their noses in his union affairs—The Chamber of Commerce, Manufacturers' Association or Merchants group—BUT THAT'S A DIFFERENT MATTER!

He knows there is a law protecting the workers' right to organize, BUT AFTER ALL, MAYBE THE WORKERS DON'T KNOW THEIR RIGHTS and besides, THERE ARE EXPERTS TO HELP HIM "BEND" THE LAW A LITTLE AS HE TRIES TO "INFLUENCE" HIS EMPLOYEES.

In recent years the pattern of company interference in union campaigns has become very common; common because it happens frequently and because it takes much the same form each time. Since it could happen here, since it *will* happen here if your employer has decided to go allout in fighting your intent to organize. You should know what sort of anti-union propaganda blockbusters the boss may start dropping in his campaign to convince you that you don't want or need a union.

LOOK OUT FOR "LOVE LETTERS" FROM the boss. All of a sudden you may be favored by a burst of affection from the boss. For the very first time since you began to work for the company, the boss may start sending letters to your home. From these letters, designed to be read both by you and your family, you will learn for the first time how "deeply concerned" he is about your welfare.

You may not have suspected it before from the size of your paycheck, but these letters will reveal that the boss worries about your economic well being. You'll discover another phase of his interest in your welfare: He is anxious that you not get mixed up with any "shady characters"—like union representatives, for instance! He may even describe them as crooks, mobsters or racketeers in his effort to convince you that they are shady characters.

Furthermore, he has a great fear that you might lose your independence and become a slave to some labor "boss" who can order you out on strike at any moment even against your will!

The letters, of course, will forget to inform you that there are some 125,000 union contracts governing labor-management relations and that 97% of them are signed after peaceful negotiations. They'll forget to mention that more workers miss work because of colds than because of strikes and that strikes have to be authorized by the workers themselves before they can be conducted.

You will learn, however, from the love letters the boss sends, that you are all part of a happy family at work and you will read his fervent hope that no foreign influence like the union will ever break up that wonderful, intimate relationship he says you've always enjoyed.

There are many, many more things the love letters will tell you. You'll enjoy reading them. You can tie them up with blue ribbon and put them in your hope chest. Hopes are about all you'll get, without a union.

LOOK OUT FOR RUMORS spread by foremen and supervisors. You may hear that raises are coming, if only that union doesn't get in. You'll hear that the boss knows whom he can trust and who is a union-sympathizer. You will hear that those who are backing the union have always been trouble-makers who have never carried their share of the work.

You may hear that the boss has his eye on you; that he has been thinking about giving you a raise or a promotion. Or you may hear that he is wondering about you and just can't believe that you would be disloyal.

You may hear that the boss is thinking of moving the company to another city or state if the workers vote for the union or that he has told a close business friend that he just will not be able to get along with the union and will probably have to shut down!

You may hear that the union will demand industry-wide seniority, and that if a union place up north or down south has a layoff, the union will shift those workers here and bump you out of a job!

LOOK OUT FOR COMMITTEES OF LOYAL EMPLOYEES that suddenly come into existence and start issuing letters and leaflets urging you to "stick with the boss." You will notice that these employees speak openly during working hours, use their names on handbills and appear to be conducting their own campaign; they are just interested workers, so they say!

LOOK OUT FOR SPECIAL COMMITTEES of local business men and civic leaders. These special committees also spring up overnight, like the special committee of loyal employees described above. This newborn committee will claim that it is interested only in your welfare when it urges you to help keep "those dirty unions" out of the community. Again, like the committee of loyal employees, this group will insist it has no connection with the company.

And don't be surprised if some members of this special committee of interested citizens call upon members of your family, to urge them to ask you not to vote for the union.

LOOK OUT FOR SPECIAL MEETINGS CALLED BY THE BOSS. The best name for these meetings is "captive audience meetings." They'll be held on company time and will feature a little homey chat from the boss himself. It may be the first time he's ever felt moved to call you together that way, at his expense, but he'll do it now, because he feels that it is so important that you know the facts of life or understand his problems. He'll remind you of all he and the company have done for you and your community; he'll tell you that you and the company are partners in a great enterprise and that you will make progress together. But he'll sadly inform you that there won't be any more togetherness if you decide to join that outside union.

If he follows the pattern, he'll suggest that a vote for the union is a vote to destroy the company and your job. He won't attempt to explain how that fits in with the fact that over 14 million American workers belong to AFL-CIO unions and the companies for which they work seem to be flourishing! Your employer may use any, or all, of these various devices—letters, rumors, threats, phony committees, captive meetings—and others not mentioned here in his attempt to convince you that you don't want or don't need a union. All of these methods are contained in standard propaganda packages developed and sold by professional union-busting specialists who are paid, and paid well, to confuse workers and get them to vote against their own best interests.

How Good is Your Job?

	Yes	No

1. Do you know your job classification?
2. Do you know whether you are being paid as much as other people doing the same job you are?
3. Do you know how the company arrived at your job classification and pay scale?
4. Do you have a remedy (short of quitting) if you are dissatisfied?
5. Do you know if your job description correctly lists the work you are supposed to be doing?
6. Are your washrooms kept spotlessly clean?
7. Do you get time-and-a-half for a *fifth* day worked if a holiday falls during the week?
8. Do you know that vacations, sick leave, etc., will always continue at the present rate?
9. Do you get overtime payments for all additional time worked in excess of 8 hours per day?
10. Do you get extra pay for work on Saturday or Sunday, as such?
11. Do you have the right to petition for a better job that is open?
12. Do you know when there are job openings?
13. Do you have security, knowing that when business slackens, layoffs will be made by seniority?
14. Do you know you will be trained for available jobs when automated systems are introduced?

IF YOU HAVE MORE THAN TWO *NO* ANSWERS, YOU OWE IT TO YOURSELF TO SIGN THAT CARD TODAY!

Figure 6.2. A job conditions questionnaire put out by a union organizing department.

Don't let some highly paid specialist tell you how to think. Don't be tricked into voting against yourself.

While you're waiting for election day, the day you make the great decision, keep looking out for the blockbusters. They're almost bound to come.

Then, on election day, look for the union box on the ballot and vote for your AFL-CIO union.

Do You Have Troubles?
A particularly effective union handout piece is the job conditions questionnaire. These make good check lists for supervisors, things that must not be permitted to exist. Figure 6.2 is the kind that is put out by a union organizing department. It will be much more effective when the questions are tilted to ask about the failings of the particular company—failings which have been uncovered in the exploratory phase of the campaign.

For Women Only
The early union communications may have a small target. In this one the woman employee is the subject of the organizer's attention:

For Women Only
A Special Message on the Advantages of a Union Contract

WOMEN PERFORM IMPORTANT FUNCTIONS IN AN OFFICE WORKFORCE. In most cases, female employees have at least a high school education and many have college or business school training. Whether they are engaged in secretarial, typing, accounting, filing or clerical work, their training proves a valuable asset to the employer.

Yes, more than ever, female employees are an important cog in the business office!

DO WOMEN RECEIVE EQUAL TREATMENT? Highly capable and well educated females are continually bypassed for promotion in favor of new male employees hired from the street.

In recognition of this inequity, the United States Congress passed laws in recent years making it compulsory for a company to give greater recognition to their female employees and to pay equal wages for equal work as well as to eliminate discrimination.

The laws were initiated and supported by labor unions. The Women's Department of _____ Union was very instrumental in pushing the legislation through Congress.

Without the ever watching eye of a union, however, most employers are able to use loopholes in the law to skirt around its provisions.

SECURITY—WHAT DOES IT MEAN TO WOMEN? The day is long gone when women look upon their jobs as a "lark" or "something to keep them busy." Women are becoming increasingly aware of the need to belong to a union and to be protected on their jobs. Over 200,000 women are members of _____ and this number is growing daily. Hundreds of women members hold union offices and make an important contribution to their union.

WHAT DOES A 'CONTRACT' MEAN? A contract covers wages, hours and conditions of employment and all aspects of an employee's relationship with the employer. Union salaried contracts include minimum and maximum wage rates for all classifications; automatic wage increases; procedure for continuation of salary during absence from work; provisions for payment of overtime rates; seniority clauses that are non-discriminatory; clauses which protect the female's seniority rights during pregnancy leaves, sick leaves and for other reasons. These provisions are spelled out in a contract book and every employee knows his or her rights.

In the absence of a contract, each employee is forced to accept, without question, conditions of employment and wages that are determined solely by their employer. The only alternative to accepting is quitting!

WHAT DOES UNION MEMBERSHIP MEAN? In a by-gone era, women were led to believe that it was undignified for them to belong and be active in a union. This myth evaporated when school teachers, screen actresses, radio and TV performers and women in other professions proudly carried union membership cards.

Today, the working girl's best friend is her union. And her best protector is her union contract!

GUARD YOUR JOB BY SIGNING A CARD AND VOTING "YES"

Dignity of Man

In the preliminary stages of the open campaign, the supervisor may find that his people are receiving handbills or letters that refer to a strange kind of dignity acquired by becoming a member of a crowd!

Every man likes to think he is important. He likes to be proud of his name, whether it is Jones or Smith or Kallalowski or any one of a million more.

He likes to be proud of himself as a man.

But in these days, it seems that more and more is being taken away from the dignity of the individual. Machines are getting

more and more important and life is a lot more complicated than
it used to be. It is getting so that the average man sometimes
feels like just one little cog in a vast machine, instead of like a
man.

In this machine age, one of the few forces working for man is
the labor union. The constant, eternal goal of _____ Union is
to protect the interests of the individual man. The union places
the human rights of man above the rights of machinery, profits
and property.

In _____, the individual man has a place to voice his
opinions, to protect his own interests. The men in the union are
banded together to use their combined strength for the welfare
of men in the machine age.

With a union, a man has a chance to keep some of his individual human dignity.

Sign Up Fast!

As the authorization card-signing campaign comes to a close, good
things are happening all over and the quicker the cards are signed, the
sooner the goodies will be available here:

We are getting wage offers from several of our Companies.
We know that the minute we petition for an election. The company is going to call you in and give you a wage increase. We
have been in negotiations now for wages since the first of the
year, and things are beginning to break. Our _____ group of
_____ Co., was offered 2¢ across the board plus 4%, with
some retroactivity.

Hurry up and sign a card, so that you won't be late on any
settlement which is made. As we have said the quicker we get an
election, the quicker the company will pass some increase on to
you. We will bet they do it just before the election to try to show
you that you don't need a union.

Demand for Recognition

As the campaign moves along and enjoys some success the
organizer will, at some point, go on with the next step, the demand for
an election:

The National Labor Relations Board has at last set the date
for hearing on the Union's petition for an election at your plant.
The hearing is now set for Monday, and will be held in _____.

As expected the company has stalled at every opportunity and we are sure they will continue to do everything they can to postpone a democratic election conducted by the government in your plant.

The fact remains that in spite of all the stalling they can do *THERE WILL BE AN ELECTION* and it will be a *SECRET BALLOT ELECTION*. It will be conducted by the National Labor Relations Board, an agency of the *U.S. GOVERNMENT.*

The company's stalling tactics of course are aimed at delaying such an election, hoping that you will become discouraged and give up your attempts to have a Union of your own.

Dues

Around the time an election is scheduled the issues become more sharply drawn. The company has made much of the need to pay dues as a reason for voting NO:

> Dues? Yes, what about it? Assume, for example, that your local will decide on $5 a month for dues. Of that, $2.50 will go to the International Union. Most of this $2.50 goes to pay for representatives who help local unions in negotiations, settling grievances and organizing. The rest is spent to pay for a legal staff to represent the interests of the members in courts and before government agencies, to pay for research experts to supply facts and figures for bargaining with your company; to pay for a twice-monthly newspaper to keep you posted on what your union is doing all across this country and Canada; and 10% of this $2.50 goes into a defense fund to support members who vote to go on strike.
>
> The other $2.50 of your $5.00 dues will stay in your local treasury, to be spent as the local members see fit on the various things a local can do.
>
> For $5.00 a month dues (a bit more than 3¢ per hour) your local will get $30 a year, the International $30 a year and you will get higher wages, better conditions and the security that comes with a written, guaranteed contract.

We Like Our Union

Glowing recommendations and tributes from other unions become available for reprint by the organizer:

> We have heard of your efforts to form a Union at Peerless. We, as fellow workers, would like to assure you that we are with

you all the way. The advantages we have gained through organization are too numerous to name. Some of you may remember when barber shops stayed open until 12 o'clock on Saturday nights and even opened on Sunday. The prices received for haircuts were 25¢ and even 15¢. Through organization we are now making a decent living and only working five days per week. Also, for the first time in history, we barbers, through our International Union, have a health and welfare plan which takes care of our hospital and doctor bills.

We urge you to vote for your union in the coming election. If we can be of any assistance, please call on us.

Get a Contract

One of the basic claims a union can put forward is the guarantee of benefits contained in the company-union labor agreement:

We think the average employee at the Plant has sense enough to evaluate the plant superintendent's letter; so therefore we don't want to discuss it further. However before we leave this discussion, we want to ask you to read your working rules and make note that at the end of the book the company states that the company can change them at any time they see fit. THEY CAN'T DO THIS IN A UNION CONTRACT. So therefore you have more security with a contract.

Exploiting Weaknesses

In the now hotter campaign, flaws in the company's personnel program are mercilessly exposed:

IT IS A FACT THAT you have only a one-man safety department in your plant? That although your working rules state you should go to First Aid every time you suffer even a minor injury, some foremen talk you out of it as they do not want lost time charged to their department? IS IT not a fact that there have been occasions lately when workers came in contact with acid and requested permission to go to First Aid and were REFUSED? The answer is YES. Haven't there been accidents lately regarding egress from box cars when men have been injured (one of them with a sprained ankle) and were made to work out the shift by the slave-driver on loading dock? The answer is YES.

'Taint so

The company has been bearing down on the strike threat; the union reacts:

> Much has been said about Unions striking. In the Union, the only people who can call a strike is the membership of the local and then it must be by secret ballot. The International Union or myself CANNOT put you on a strike. Anytime you hear of a strike, remember that the employees voted for it. Our plants in _____ enjoy great progress and without strikes. No one wants a strike and again I say, the employees must make such a decision, not the International Union. The _____ Union is one of the few that pays its members if they vote to strike, by the week. Also, the employees do not pay their monthly dues, the stamps are free.

The Best People

As the election nears, the union's emphasis shifts from recruiting new supporters to consolidating the support already signed up. Communicating continues in all channels, perhaps including a full-page ad in the local newspaper. It is pointed more toward strengthening a pro-union feeling than to rounding up new union voters:

**Great Men Agree . . . Unions are Good
are Superior's Workers Asking too Much?**

FOR THE RIGHT TO enjoy a decent standard of living which could provide the necessities of life for their families?

TO BE TREATED AS first-class citizens?

TO EXPECT SECURITY on their jobs and thereby plan for a brighter tomorrow?

TO PROVIDE for homes, education for their children, cars, proper medical care without the burden of mortgage?

TO EXPECT management to provide basic protection against safety hazards and in-plant medical care?

Only the Superior workers can know the answers to these and many more questions affecting their daily livelihood. Not the so-called "industrial committee" thing nor the well-fed Chamber of Commerce. Superior workers should be permitted to work as citizens, not servants.

SUPERIOR WORKERS WILL VOTE FOR _____ UNION
WEDNESDAY, JULY 2

Dwight D. Eisenhower—"Only a fool would try to deprive working men and working women of the right to join the union of their choice."

Harry S. Truman—"The right to join a union of one's choice is unquestioned today and is sanctioned and protected by law."

John F. Kennedy—"The American labor movement has consistently demonstrated its devotion to the public interest. It is, and has been, good for all America."

Franklin D. Roosevelt—"If I were a worker in a factory, the first thing I would do would be to join a union."

Signed: (Organizing Committee)

The union, by probing, will find most of the weaknesses and it will exploit them to the hilt. Many union campaigners try to communicate constantly with new handbills, letters and posters daily. So the sampling here is not representative of a union campaign on a basis of sheer volume.

Again, these ideas are all the more forceful to workers because they come, not only from printed materials and in meetings run by the organizer, but from trusted and well-liked fellow workers on the job and off.

Chapter 7
The Company Communicates Ideas

Powerful as the union message seems, the employer has a message at least as powerful. Employers are winning about half of the elections that are held. Remember that these are the cases that unions have chosen to take to the point of an election, thinking they can win. The evidence is that the company can win the battle of ideas if it is able to communicate its point of view. Larger units tend to vote pro-company, likely because ideas, rather than personal pressures, prevail in the larger groups of workmen.

In the union-sponsored survey that demonstrated the importance of face-to-face contacts in the union campaign, one question asked what technique of management had influenced their voting most strongly. Again, the top two methods mentioned were face-to-face: first rated was the top executive "captive audience" speech; second was talks by supervisors or foremen with small groups of employees. The third one mentioned was employer letters to the home.

The supervisor's role is once more spotlighted. The captive audience speech is a one-shot affair, the kind of thing that is apt to come to mind when a person is pressed for an answer. Not so spectacular is the day-to-day shaping of attitudes by the supervisor in meetings and in one-on-one conversation. Studies made by a large manufacturer showed that the people at the lowest level of skill scarcely relied on the written word for news, entertainment, company information or anything else. They relied mainly on the spoken word (and for entertainment, spent a much higher percent of their time listening to TV than people at higher education and skill levels). As for written company communication, it was found that many were only headline readers. The supervisor must not assume that his people want to get their information in the same form as he does.

The union survey looked into the reasons ranked most powerful in causing a pro-company vote. First ranked is paying dues and second, "the union was not needed." These summarize the two main arguments of management: the union system is undesirable, certainly not worth paying dues for, and the company provides a work experience that makes a union simply irrelevant.

The union's findings about what type of person voted pro-union gives the supervisor a lead on where his emphasis should be in the campaign. It will be remembered that women were somewhat more inclined to vote for a union than men. Young workers showed no important tendency. The survey also showed there was no important difference between single and married workers. Significantly, *workers with more than a year of service and less than ten years were much more apt to be anti-union* than workers with shorter or longer service. Previous union membership was a factor in voting for a union; almost a third of all those who voted pro-union had been union members some time previously.

The survey, to the surprise of practically no one, found that workers with conservative views were more inclined than those with liberal political ideas (progressive, as the union survey put it) to vote for the company. Another finding of the survey was that the pro-company worker somehow did not have as much strength of character as the pro-union because he "wavered", tended to change his mind one or more times in the campaign. Couldn't this be better described as "open-minded?"

To keep the subject of company communicating in the proper light, it must be said again that actions and words over the long run are first in importance; the close relationship that yields communication upward is the key. An analysis of 135 elections made by an employer group revealed that in 68 cases the employer learned about the union organizing activity through his employees; in the other 67 cases the activity was disclosed by the union or by the NLRB when the union requested the election. Where the employer had learned of the drive from his employees, he won 76% of the elections that followed. Where the company learned from the union or the NLRB, it won in only 37% of the elections.

It is hardly necessary to add that early notice of union activity may be more *effect* than *cause*. It is true that the company can swing into its counter-campaign and correct ills in its employee relations program, hardly possible when the union has given notice of its presence. But more important, it indicates that the rapport is there that will give early warning. It may also mean that many employees so oppose unionism that they report union activity in anger.

But the union is here and the supervisor asks, "What can I say?" The short answer is that he can say what his management asks him to say. For several good reasons an employer may ask his supervisors to limit their discussion of union matters with the employees. This is a management decision. Such a decision to forego the communication power of the first-line leader is usually taken only on expert advice and the leader must respect it.

Many NLRB cases can be found in which there is a sharp conflict of witnesses as to what a supervisor actually said in talks with employees about unionism. His exact words are in question. He will usually be outnumbered by the union's employee-witnesses and the conflict is often resolved in favor of the union. This prompts many companies to instruct their supervisors not to enter such discussions during a union organizing campaign unless another member of management is present.

There are a great variety of subjects the company can use, as the situation dictates. The company's whole approach may be different if the organization move is clearly coming from the outside, the union having descended on the company with little or no initial support from within. All the employees will know this, whether they are involved with the union or not, and the company needs to know, so that its communications will be credible and its campaign plan sound. This is a key item of information that good supervisor-employee rapport will turn up.

The management statements offered here are taken from letters, leaflets and speeches, but are not identified as such to avoid leaving the impression that a certain type of communication should be used. The content is the important thing and study of the examples will give the supervisor a good guide as to the types of reasoning and arguments he may use, with no great risk of violating the law or upsetting the Board's election rules (this, however, should not be regarded as legal advice; the legality of a statement or communication should be obtained from legal counsel).

Throughout these discussions the company is Superior. Superior is an office, a plant, a store or any business and seems to be found in many industries. None of these thoughts was actually said or written by a Superior, unless coincidentally. Using the familiar name of our company, Superior, rather than inventing a full corporate name, is no accident. This is the best way to refer to the company in a written piece, according to skilled communicators. Never say "the company" if it can be avoided. To some it is a red cape. This advice holds good for the spoken word: make it "Superior" or if the meaning won't suffer, "we."

There are several ways to classify campaign messages for study. The two major themes are the undesirability of having a union in the plant and the benefits that the company offers without a union. Another way to look at it is in terms of the campaign: the different kinds of subjects that are covered in the early maneuvering, the hot campaigning and the final days of the campaign. Here, we will look at the things that are said as we progress through the campaign, taking a close look at the major themes in the hot campaigning:

The Early Maneuvering

An important burden of the company's early communication after open campaigning begins is feeding back accurate news along promptly. It is also appropriate here to give the employees an idea of the company's general position and what is to be expected in the way of union tactics. The following message reports the news in a light that is favorable to the company; first, the union will be making loose promises and the presence of a union can bring strikes:

The NLRB hearing is behind us. As you know, last month this union demanded that we let it bargain for our operating people as well as the smaller maintenance group it has been representing. We refused, feeling it was unfair to allow the destinies of the operating group to be dictated by the results of an election held years before, in which they did not participate.

This union saw nothing unfair about it and petitioned the NLRB for an election in a group composed of operating and maintenance people. This would throw into the results a bloc of maintenance votes they think they control.

In the hearing concluded yesterday the lines were drawn on this point. We believed our operating people should be allowed to decide their representation for themselves. The union demanded that both groups be forced to vote together. The matter now lies with the Board for decision.

You will hear plenty from the union in the next weeks. They will be promising you everything they think you want to hear: more pay, more benefits, more security and less work.

WHEN YOU HEAR THESE PROMISES, ASK YOURSELF HOW MUCH THEY ARE WORTH. A union can PROMISE anything, but can they deliver? They can only present their promises to Superior as demands. If Superior does not acquiesce, the union can strike.

Nobody wants a strike. For Superior it means loss of revenue; for you men, loss of pay and sometimes loss of your job. Only the union officials are unaffected, since their pay goes on as if nothing had happened.

None of us want this threat hanging over us. An outsider is not needed to run your affairs at Superior. Accordingly, we plan from time to time to keep you informed of news in this case and to speak our minds, sincerely and forthrightly, on unionism.

The early maneuvering is a good time for the more general messages. These arguments can be prepared well in advance by the campaign task force. A very special appeal to groups such as "knowledge" workers, technicians, or office workers is the idea that they are not the union type:

> You are hearing a lot of noise about job security from the paid organizers. They seem to think that "security" is the magic password to longer checkoff lists of dues payers.
>
> If you were house-wiring men or construction workers, the type of labor this International customarily handles, you would likely be fascinated by a promise of JOB SECURITY. But you have a skill that is in demand; you are not married to Superior. The organizers' security talk is for the mill hand, who must turn to a union for his job. You are here because this was the best job available to you in this area and we intend to keep you here on the same basis.

A specific warning about the dangers of signing authorization cards is usually a good idea. If the union is unsuccessful in getting 50% to 70% of the group signed up, it very likely will not move on to an election event though only 30% is needed to prove a "show of interest" to the NLRB and have a Board-conducted election. The supervisor should know about the dangers of these cards. The organizers will imply that they are only to be used to get a secret ballot election (appealing to the employees' sense of fair play) when in fact they can be used in a number of ways to nullify a lost election or bypass an election completely:

> These people will be asking you to sign their application card to get a secret ballot election. They will go on to say that the company never sees the cards which they want you to sign.

This is an insult to your intelligence. Read the card, it doesn't say anything about getting a secret ballot election. It is an application for membership in their union. It appoints them as your exclusive agent, meaning it would take away from you your individual right to discuss your problems with management and would place this right in the hands of outsiders.

They will often show these cards to the company in a demand that the company recognize their union so they won't have to have an election. They often show these cards to other employees and to people all over town. They may put them in evidence in a formal hearing of the NLRB and the one who signed the card may be called on the witness stand to testify.

They will tell you that you are the only one in your group holding out, to try to get you to jump on the band wagon. Another insult to your intelligence.

Just tell them you will make up your mind when an election is held, but you won't sign a card. You have a legal right not to sign these cards.

If you have any questions about these cards, your rights, the law, or anything about the union's campaign, ask me. I will give you the answer or find the answer for you.

A communication about authorization cards invites questions from the workers. The supervisor should arm himself with the facts, when his company wants him to communicate, and be prepared to pass them on. He must never question his people about their union beliefs or about the union's campaign and he must not spy. But he can talk, either to groups or person-to-person, and he can answer questions. He can listen.

A fine point: there is a distinct difference, in the eyes of the NLRB, between interviewing people at their place of work or in open areas and interviewing in the supervisor's or manager's office. Taking a man to the office or the "seat of authority" to press a pro-company view is considered a type of coercion and should not be done.

When the Election is Scheduled

In the hotter campaigning that takes place after an election is scheduled the company will usually unlimber all of its artillery. We can expect to see three general approaches to persuading people to mark the NO UNION box on the ballot: the ill effects of unionism; advantages of dealing with the company direct; and a mixture of these in the infighting and information-handling of the campaign.

III Effects of Unionism

Unrest and Discontent

Men who have never worked in a union environment will have noticed the new air of dissension and discontent since the union appeared. Unless a vivid picture of everyday life with a union is presented they may believe that the union will bring some kind of workers' paradise, worth a few sacrifices. A note, too, about the inside "clique" of company employees who will have positions of power if the union wins—a most effective note when this group is not a particularly popular one:

> They are at work among you right now to spread discontent with your situation, these paid organizers and a small partisan nucleus of your fellow employees. This bloc can be depended upon to vote for the union no matter what facts are brought out. By spreading discontent they hope to scatter your votes so that their bloc vote can seize control. They will be your overlords if the union ever gets in.
>
> Clearheaded folks don't like trouble and bickering. For this reason, the International Representatives play down the strikes, upheaval, distrust and dissension that exist in unionized plants.
>
> They soft-pedal the discontent and the perpetual unrest that goes on. It is easy to picture the bitterness that goes with a strike, and none of us want this. The thing about union life that is not so well known is the constant squabbling between workers, and between worker and foreman that goes on every day.
>
> And most of it is deliberately inspired by the union! Only if there is griping and discontent with the management or the foremen can a union justify its existence. They are literally merchants of discontent.

Union Promises

As in the warnings about signing authorization cards and the description of life in a unionized plant, an employer owes it to his people to warn them about union promises in the campaign. Otherwise, the fact that a union can promise and a company can't could affect the outcome of the election:

> Let's discuss some of the NLRB ground rules that apply to a union's organizing attempt.

A company *cannot promise* you anything or threaten you in connection with how you vote. But on the other hand, *the union can promise* you the moon. This is one-sided, but there is some wisdom in it: you are expected to know that the union cannot make good on a promise about wages, hours or working conditions. Any such benefit must be given by the employer. Of course, the union can pull you out on strike to try to make good on its demands.

So the paid International Union organizers will come to you with promises and criticisms of Superior. The criticisms you should judge for yourself. You know more about Superior and its people than a paid organizer from outside the state will ever know.

Their promises are something else. There is no way to guess what they will promise, to get your dues, assessments and initiation fees.

Take wages, for instance. They tell you there are higher rates paid for your work, in other parts of the nation. We don't know where they get their information, but we can show you many lower ones than ours. The real comparison should be with wages paid here. Make your own wage comparison. You know people who do the same work you do, in other companies. Ask them.

Don't feel sorry for the organizers. They are getting used to being told to look elsewhere for dues payers. More and more workers are voting NO to union organizing raids. *Plan now to vote NO when election day rolls around!*

Job Security

One of the union's most potent promises is a guarantee of job security. It boils down to a form of protection against unfair discharge, and layoffs and promotions by seniority. This is not the real security, however, and the company is quick to point it out:

Job Security! What job can be more secure than the firm which created that job? To promise job security is one thing. To deliver it is another. A union promises it freely, but all it can do to deliver it is to make a demand backed up by the threat of a strike.

The very purpose of a strike is to bring a company to its knees. It is not hard to imagine what a long drawn-out strike can do to the security of the jobs that company has created.

But suppose the company does not take the strike lying down. In an economic strike the company can go right out and hire new men, permanently, in the jobs the strikers have deserted. You have seen this happen. You may know men who are out of work today because they were taken out on strike. This is security?

The union idea of security can be summed up, "More People Doing Less Work." I cannot imagine a graver threat to the security of Superior and to your job.

Wipe out this threat. Vote NO on Friday.

Loss of the Personal Touch

This is a continuation of the theme that life in the plant will not be better, but worse, if a union is on the scene:

> You may ask, why should I buy something here that my common sense tells me I don't want? So many others have done it? In the old unionized plants it's a different thing. The people are different. They don't know the foreman, the supervisor or even their fellow employees. They pay to have somebody deal with the company.
>
> With a union you surrender your rights to discuss your problems with us. In fact, you pay a party from out of town to tell us about your problems. Let's reverse this. If I had a problem that concerned you, what would your reaction be to my going out of town, and hiring a stranger you didn't know to approach you about our mutual problem?
>
> A union would create division among you. The same leaders, the same feelings, the same tactics that exist in a campaign still exists after a union is voted in. Luckily, we have a right-to-work law in this state and no one can be forced to join a union in order to work. No one can lose his job because he hasn't signed a pledge card. Don't let anyone tell you differently.

Worsen a Bad Financial Situation

A company need not pull any punches if its financial situation is perilous. An employee is not well served if he believes things are rosy and going well for the company when in fact they were not:

> Superior is the sole source of supply for many of our customers. They would worrry about the strikes. They would say, "We'd better split our business with at least one other company."

Which outcome in the election will best help jobs and the business? Our losses have been substantial. We have been fighting, so far successfully, a real battle for survival. You can see the sudden effect that a union win may have on jobs and work in the plant, because what's good for the company and its employees will take second place to what's good for the union and its business agents.

Regardless of the outcome of the election we are going to do our best to make Superior a strong and stable company. We do not intend to become a statistic. But Superior has earned money *in only two of the ten years of its existence.*

Something to Lose

In seeking members, organizers will play upon the theme that an employee has everything to gain and nothing to lose by joining a union. He does have many things to lose and here are a couple of them:

The union can promise anything, but can it deliver? The fact is it may not be able to keep all the things you already have. No one can assume that if an outside union gets into our company that all the fine things we now enjoy will automatically be continued. If Superior should be forced into negotiating with a union, we would bargain hard to protect our competitive position.

Wherever it controls employees' affairs, the _____ Union always tries to get the union shop. In a union shop, every employee must join the union.

An employee can be fined by the union and the union can collect in court, just like it was a debt. If he falls behind in his dues the company must fire him on request of the union.*

The employee has no say in the matter. Your freedom of choice is taken away by the iron-fisted domination of the union shop.

The Union Clique

The leadership that the union has chosen will clearly be the crown princes if the union takes over. If the inside group is clannish the idea

---

* This is true only where the union contract requires this and in states where such contracts are lawful.

that these insiders have a special self-interest in a union win will have strong appeal to the others. The following message is backed by language from a contract of the union covering another group of workers.

Are the organizers interested in only a few? What are their promises to this little clique?

Here is a quote from a contract of this International Union with an upstate company.

Seniority of Union Representatives

Official representatives of the Union shall have various superseniority rights defined below in the event of layoffs or recall. Employees having such superseniority rights shall include the president, one vice-president, chief steward, one assistant chief steward, one treasurer, one recording secretary, one financial secretary, one sergeant at arms, three trustees, nine committeemen and not more than one steward for every 25 employees in the bargaining unit. Superseniority shall mean a seniority that is *greater* than *any seniority achieved by length of employment.*

This means that a man with one day's service as a union officer and as little as one year of plant seniority can, in time of layoff, take another man's job even though the second man has 30 year's plant seniority.

The Strike Threat

To the non-union worker the strike is the one facet of union life that is easily understood and is to be feared. It is the issue that the company and the employee have in common as a reason for avoiding the union's advances.

Don't you know that the Union positively cannot force or compel any company to give fantastic increases in wages? What they *can* do is take the employees out on strike to *attempt* to force the company to give increases. You might as well know now, we will take a strike before we will give any fantastic increases in wages.

We have taken strikes in New Albany, Indiana, for several months and a strike in Port Arthur, Texas, that began in November 14, 1970, and is still not settled.

Strikes hurt everybody except the Union organizers. The company loses sales and the employees lose wages. No striker can expect to regain his lost wages through increases gained by striking.

Another thing, a striker might very well lose his job in an economic strike because the company can go right out and permanently hire an outsider and give that person the job of the striker.

The talk can get very frank, even brutal, about strikes. This is not the legal risk that other subjects may become, since strikes are obviously not within the company's control. A strike prediction cannot be classified as an illegal threat:

Unions mean strikes. This union was involved in 11 major strikes in the Los Angeles area alone during the past two years. Unions are warring organizations. We would regret seeing any of you tramping picket lines out at the street, with payless paydays. Try and name one place in L. A. with an outside union where there hasn't been a strike. Union leaders have a talent for stirring up trouble and creating dissension and bitterness.

How many of you have worked in a union plant? Was it all a bed of roses? Or were there layoffs, strikes, reprimands, firing, gripes, complaints, and dissatisfaction? And if you go on strike, how long will you have to work to make up for that loss of pay?

Do you want to continue the Superior way of harmony, friendship and person-to-person dealings or do you want to bring into this plant an outside union which will bring strikes, bickering, hard feelings, and trouble? All of this subsidized by your hard-earned cash taken out of your paycheck before you even see it?

A lofty approach to strikes may have a profound effect on workers as they reach an understanding of the variety of strikes that can blight a peaceful existence:

What is a sympathy strike?

It is defined as a work stoppage by the employees of one employer to express solidarity with striking employees of another employer, to exert indirect pressure on the latter management.

It is a situation where your union sees another union striking and thinks it would be a great idea if you struck in sympathy with that other union. You have no quarrel with your company and may have no acquaintances in this other union, but there you are out on the bricks, not working and not being paid.

Strikes come in all shapes and sizes. There is the *industry-wide strike* in which all the organized workers in a particular industry go out; the *jurisdictional strike* which results from a jurisdictional dispute between unions; the *secondary strike* in which a strike is called against one employer with a view of influencing another; the *whipsaw strike* in which a union stages successive strikes on different employers. Most of them are for the benefit of unions, not workers.

And all of them for unionized people, not union-free, as we are here.

It is hard to say too much about strikes in a campaign to fight off the union:

> Let's talk about strikes for a moment. We know that *strike* is an ugly word, but if you vote for this union, remember that the strike is the only weapon that a union has to try to force Superior to give in to its demands.
>
> We don't like strikes. We don't like strikes because they put friend against friend, and neighbor against neighbor. Strikes cost a company money through lost production. Strikes cost a community money through lost buying power; strikes cost the workers money through lost wages, and most of all, strikes breed ill will, hatred and bad feeling. Strikes can happen here.
>
> You have been told by the union organizers that only you can call a strike and that it is very unlikely for you to have a strike. *But you must understand* that unions take strike votes frequently that are meaningless. The union can call a meeting to vote on a strike at which only a few people are present. This could mean that a mere handful of rabid union supporters could vote you out on a strike.
>
> Again, a union will often tell the membership that they need a strike vote to be able to get a better bargain with the company by having the strike for a threat. The first thing you know, you are carrying a poster.
>
> Don't be misled by assurances of these union professionals that you will probably not be called out on strike. Last year, nearly 2½ million workers were put out of work because of strikes. You were not called out on strike because you did not have a union *It's the only sure way.*

Union Violence

The brutality and violence that often reach the headlines in connection with union activities is a side of unionism that workers are entitled to see. Letters and mailings on this subject can be accompanied by photos and copies of clippings from newspapers.

To gain all these benefits neither you nor I have ever missed one single paycheck, have never been told to stay home one single day. In fact, you have never missed one hour of work as a result of any action by Superior. You haven't had to strike, walk a picket line or engage in bitter quarrels with Superior. You have not had to give up any rights to any outsiders and strangers.

We got these things by working close together, doing an efficient job and helping the plant to operate on a profitable basis.

May I urge that you not take these things lightly. We have not had the trouble and hatred and suspicion which outsiders have caused in so many other places. We haven't had production interrupted by gas lines being bombed, machinery being sabotaged, automobiles being overturned, your neighbors houses being bombed, wives being threatened, or children being scared.

These things have happened, and *are happening*, in places not far from here. We don't want them to happen in _____. Not just because it would involve Superior and the community, but because it involves your relationship with your fellow employees. It involves your wife. It involves your children.

Advantages of Dealing With the Company

On the positive side, there is much to be said for maintaining the direct relationship between worker and management. Communication on this subject usually takes the form of listing benefits gained without the assistance of a union. The following is a letter which violates the otherwise good advice to make letters no longer than a page and a half. It is long, but this only emphasizes the many benefits available without the help of a union.

Don't stand back and let others decide your future for you. When you *do not* vote, the effect may be a vote for the Union. The election will be decided by the majority of the votes cast. So the election can be won by less than a majority of the people entitled to vote.

You must realize how you vote in this election is an important decision. Many times decisions are not nearly so tough when you have all the facts before you to weigh and reach a sound conclusion. Remember.
WITHOUT this International Union
WITHOUT a strike
WITHOUT any lost time
WITHOUT surrendering your rights to outsiders
YOU HAVE

Good wage rates—You already know this because you have seen your pay check grow over the last few years.

Company paid sickness benefits—Superior provides cash benefits, at no cost to you, when you are absent from work due to sickness. Benefits increase with length of service.

Nine paid holidays per year—Superior provides nine holidays with pay and you are paid double time if you are required to work on a holiday.

Paid vacations—After a year of service you are eligible for two weeks vacation with pay and after ten years you are eligible for three weeks paid vacation.

Military leave—You can attend National Guard encampments without loss in your earnings. If you are called to military service on a permanent basis you will receive a cash bonus when you enter and will be reinstated here when you leave. Your group benefits will be continued for you.

Paid jury duty leave—You are allowed to be absent to serve on a jury without loss of pay.

Paid funeral leave—You can attend the funeral of a member of your immediate family without loss of pay.

Hospitalization and surgical insurance—You and your dependents are equally eligible for this generous benefit, low-cost program.

Life insurance—Superior maintains a group life insurance program, paying the major part of the premium.

Retirement plan—Superior contributes considerably more than you toward the contributory portion of the program and pays the entire cost of the basic portion.

Periodic physical examinations—A thorough physical examination for your protection, free.

Additional pay for shift work—You receive an additional 15¢ per hour while working the evening shift and 30¢ while working graveyards.

Written working rules—A policy and practice booklet is your written guarantee of your working conditions at Superior.

Top notch first aid facilities—You have a fully equipped first aid station, ambulance and registered nurse.

Pleasant and businesslike working conditions—This you may judge for yourself.

I am sure you saw some benefits here that you had forgotten all about. These things were given to you by Superior without pressures from outsiders, without strikes, lost time or loss of pay and without surrendering any of your rights to outsiders.

I urge you to compare these benefits with those of other plants, union or non-union, with those you received from your former employer or with those your friends receive in other places of employment.

You did not need this International Union to get you your job here. You did not need this International Union to obtain the fine benefits which you now enjoy.

The company that has made a good effort to provide steady work should not be shy about claiming credit for it. Most workers will sense that the personal concern that leads the company to do this will not be there if a union lies across the communication lines:

As matters now stand, you have a good job and steady employment here at Superior with desirable earnings and many other benefits. Naturally, we all hope things will get even better and they can be better if we can get this union matter behind us and get this plant back to normal and settle down to the business for which all of us are here. Things can get better through all of us working together, as we have in the past, rather than pulling apart as this union would like to have us do.

The choice is yours, but I do sincerely hope that you will use your best judgment in making that choice. If you will study this whole matter thoroughly and think it through, I believe you too will surely come to the conclusion in your own good judgment, that you stand to lose if this union were to get in here and you stand to gain by keeping it out. You stand to gain for the simple reason that a vote against the union is a vote against the kind of trouble that this union can bring upon us.

The NLRB approved the next message as being no more than an economic prophecy. This is a different matter from describing life in a unionized workplace where the management's speculation can be nearly unrestrained. Prophecy should be handled with care, since there is always the danger that it will be seen by the Board as a threat. Note, too, that this is a two-union election. The only difference is that the employer is not permitted to support one against the other:

> The coming election will be the most important event in the career of Superior employees. Its outcome can seriously affect the future of your job. Indifference can lead to an outcome you may later regret.
>
> This election is being held to determine whether the employees wish to be represented by the CIO, the AFL or by neither. If you wish the shop to continue operating as it has in the past you should vote for NEITHER. Even if you are a member of a Union or have signed a card *you still have the right to vote NEITHER.*
>
> It is your right to join a Union and the company will not interfere with that right. But it is also your right *not* to join a Union and not to be represented by a Union. I want to be sure you understand that you cannot be forced to join a Union.
>
> Superior employees have worked for the past 25 years without the need of an outside labor organization. During this period there has been the closest cooperation between workers and management. It is this cooperation that has enabled the company to provide the steadiest employment, over good years and bad, of any foundry in the state.
>
> If the election is won by one of these Unions you lose your freedom of action. Decisions affecting your employment will be made by others, not by you. Efficient production will be handicapped by senseless restrictions. Cooperation will be replaced by disputes. Your daily newspaper tells the story.
>
> It is my honest belief that under a Union contract we would not be able to maintain the past standard of employment that has made Superior a good place to work.
>
> Failure to vote is equivalent to a vote for a Union. If you want to keep this shop on the same successful, job producing basis it has been for the past 25 years, go to the voting booth and mark your ballot with an X in the middle square, under the word NEITHER.

In the course of the campaign deficiencies in the company's employee relations program may have been exposed. It may be a good plan to admit mistakes have been made, but that by working together improvements can be made:

We all realize that you can never have a perfect situation at work. We can see that there is room for improvement, though many improvements have been made over the last few years and we are always trying to do better.

Rome wasn't built in a day and our plant is still a young one. We have a long way to go and the only way for us to get there is to meet our problems head on and overcome them one at a time. We are only human and we have made mistakes, but by working together and establishing closer relationships we can all reach our goals.

Nothing has ever been achieved by a group that was divided and we don't want our group divided now by letting some outsider tell us how things should be done here at our plant. You and I know how things should be done at our plant and we can do them without the interference of the union.

Our house is not going to be divided against itself, but is going to be built on an undivided foundation of hard work, cooperation, understanding and two-way loyalty.

The Infighting

In all stages of the campaign there is apt to be direct give-and-take in the communication battle between company and union. Usually this is the company answering a union charge or exposing "puffing" about the benefits of union life. Some company campaigners place great importance on this, establishing regular bulletin board postings or "Truth Forums" to answer the latest union propaganda.

Here is one that was written by a company in answer to a unions reply to a company statement about strikes:

You can lose your job in a strike.

One of the paid union organizers recently took exception to this fact and said that a company has no legal right to fire an employee who is on strike. This is only another example of how the union organizers will try to mislead you by playing with words.

Let's look at a real-life situation. Suppose this union gets in here, and then, in an effort to force Superior to give in to some of their contract demands, calls you out on strike. Is it important whether Superior would have the legal right to say, "You're fired," when it *does* have the right to hire someone in your place, so there is no job left for you?

A company has a perfect legal right to replace strikers in such a situation and it makes no difference whether you call it firing or replacing, you still don't have a job.

Here the union has made progress with the idea that the workers should give the union a chance to perform. The company's response is that there is almost no way out:

There is danger to all of us in the unionist's theme, "Try us out for one year only, and if we don't please you, you can send us away".

Voting a union in is not a step to be taken lightly. A union in a plant is like communism in a nation: it is not the type of thing that you can try out for a while. A union never really intends to be sent out on approval. After they take over, there are thousands of ways to put pressure on a man who shows opposition to the union leadership group that is "in".

It is very nearly a one-way street. It is a lot like one of those long-neck fish traps that the fish can get into slick as a whistle, but the fish who can wiggle his way out is lucky indeed.

Especially when it appears the company is not strongly opposed to the union, the union will sell itself by saying, "Join us—this will be something extra, a good thing, that you will have in addition to all you now have." Or they may say, "Join up—what do you have to lose?" The management answers with chapter and verse on what there is to lose:

"What do I have to lose?"

You have everything important to lose: The whole atmosphere at work here; your own right to speak for yourself in matters that involve you and the company; and if the union takes you out on strike and you are legally replaced you can even lose your job. What you are sure to gain is the added expense of dues, fines and assessments; a lot of synthetic opposition to the company; and political conniving by union cliques who are always wanting to order you or influence you to support their own views in petty union affairs.

Final Campaign

The final days of the campaign will see both sides summing up their best arguments. The company will usually urge the workers to vote, since a small turnout tends to favor the union; and will stress the fact that signing a card does not obligate the worker to vote pro-union. A manager, particularly if he is a popular one, should not hesitate to expose his feeling and personal involvement in the outcome:

Next Tuesday you will have the opportunity to decide by secret ballot whether we will continue to conduct our employee relationships as we have in the past or have the _____ Union act as bargaining agent at Superior.

I think you will be interested in knowing my feelings about all of this. I honestly believe you will be happier over the long run by working out your problems in the spirit of teamwork and cooperation that we have always enjoyed. I say a union is not the answer.

But the decision is yours. Your choice will be between the _____ and "No Union". You will vote by secret ballot. No one but you will know how you vote. No card or anything else you may have signed obligates you to vote for the union.

In deciding how you will vote, I am sure you will study the pros and cons of unionism closely. You read of charges of corruption and crime by highly placed union officials almost daily. You have seen forceful examples in the South last year of the unrest and violence and loss of pay and loss of sales that strikes can cause. Our own city has had more than its share of losses due to strikes.

None of us want this threat hanging over us. You don't need a lot of strangers to help you run your affairs at Superior. I urge you to vote "NO" Tuesday!

Last-minute communications must be responsive to the situation. This one was designed to counter a union's house-to-house campaign that seemed to be succeeding:

Wednesday is election day and I am sure many of you have not even seen the professional organizers who are seeking to expand their international union at your expense. You have only heard the rumors they have started, their self-serving promises. They have put nothing in writing. They have no position. They have not come out in the open.

This is done in a deliberate attempt to kill your interest in the election. They hope that most of you will stay away from the polls and that a very few will decide your future for you.

I urge that every one of you vote. Think carefully about all the *facts* and separate these facts from the *promises* and rumors. If you do these things, when the secret ballots are counted we will still be running our affairs on a dignified, man-to-man basis.

The union organizers will be looking somewhere else for dues dollars.

The Captive Audience

Speeches to group meetings have been effective in many company campaigns. These talks are best received when given on or near the workplace, during work hours and with pay (actually under orders to attend). Also, to avoid violating the NLRB's election rules the speech must not take place less than 24 hours before the beginning of the balloting.

Captive audience speeches may be held any time in the campaign. The audience may be only part of the voting unit. But the most often used captive audience speech is the one given 25 hours before the election, in a meeting of all employees.

In the campaign-closing speech, the management must sum up its position. For an idea of the wide range of ideas the manager and the supervisor may explore here is an address to a "captive audience":

I feel a little bit strange up here this afternoon because it will be the first time in my life that I have ever talked with you and had exactly what I was going to say written in front of me and a little black machine here to record exactly everything that I say, and I am doing this to prevent either myself or the company from being charged with law-breaking.

Last month I received a telegram saying that Joyce Norton, Cynthia Lipscomb, Naomi Russ, Stella Wilson, Mary Webb, Patsy Russell, Jane Mooney and Joan Anderson were a part of the organizational committee to secure a union here at Superior. Needless to say, this was a disappointment to me. We still have the same objections as we have had on the previous three times that the union has attempted to organize you for your dues. For some of you new ladies and men who have not been here to defeat unions in elections of the past, we would like to reiterate to you our belief.

(The speaker is the plant manager. He is standing before a lectern on a low platform in the corner of a makeshift auditorium—an unused space in the warehouse with folding chairs for the audience of about a hundred, most of them women. Four men, department heads, are seated behind him on the platform.)

First, with a union you surrender your rights to discuss your problems with us. In fact, an uninterested party from out of town tells us about your problems. Let's reverse this. You wouldn't like it if you had a problem with someone that could be settled face to face, but she went and got some stranger to talk to you about it.

Second, outside influence cannot obtain more than Superior in the past has willingly given you.

Third, a union would create a division of employees here. The same leaders, the same hard feelings, the same upsets that exist in a campaign will exist once a union is voted in.

(The others on the platform try to keep their eyes on the speaker, but their attention is obviously on the audience and its reaction to his words.)

Fourth, a union will reduce your actual true earnings through their monthly dues and other charges. I even notice that they offer the opportunity for you to pay for a physical examination by them instead of your own doctor, via a mobile truck that, by their own admission, does not even exist in this part of the country.

Fifth, we have never felt that Superior or this city was the size or place for outsiders to take away your rights. This is both a personable town and company. All of you know all of us here on the platform. In the company and community you are a real person with a name and not just a social security number.

Finally, I wonder just what is in it for those who are a part of the organizational committee.

(The audience seems cool. A small group make a show of boredom. Is it Joyce, Cynthia, Naomi and company?)

Now, in the past what has Superior done?

It has given all of us jobs and paid us regularly. As you will remember when we had to tear out the entire second floor, the company got crews to work seven days a week twenty-four hours a day, and paid you while you were off. Not only this, but Superior has always preferred to hire too few and work overtime than to hire too many and risk the possiblity of someone not having a full paycheck some week. Do you honestly think a union could make Superior do this if we didn't want to?

You have grown as Superior has grown. Pay scale, benefits, working conditions have improved as we have grown together. Superior's policy always has been to make the conditions the best we can afford when we can afford them. This we have done because we wanted to.

(One of the girls sitting near the front leans to a friend and whispers, "Boy, he's sure giving 'em what-for!")

Superior has provided a safe and a desirable place to work in a community that is excellent to raise a family. We have even moved people from machine to machine and unit to unit to keep everyone in work. It is this mutual interest that we have had for you that makes us different from the place that would send you home when either you or your section ran out of work.

You have had continuous work all year and many times at great expense. We have just been through one of these periods when you were making a lot of tailored pajamas in some oddball colors that you probably hadn't seen in years and years and some 15 denier sets. These were cut so that you would have something to do. As I understand, union plants generally shut down as soon as the work runs out.

(The mood of the audience has changed. Heads are nodding in agreement. The "bored" group is downcast.)

We have built a strong company where one does not worry about a paycheck being cashed. This is in spite of the fact that we operate differently from most lingerie makers. Before we ever receive an order from an independent customer, we buy hundreds of thousands of dollars of piece goods and trims so that we can keep you working. This is all done before the customer sees a sample. Would you risk this if there was an uncertain relationship between you and me?

Now, for the record, what can the union do and what can it not do? There are three things a union can do. a) It can charge you dues. As I understand, the regular monthly dues are $4.00 a month at present. The union may pour these dues into supporting political candidates you are against. b) They can call you out on strike. In either case it costs you money. The union didn't pay those who went on strike for three years at a garment company some thirty miles from here. Who lost? c) They can talk to the company about your problems but you can do that yourself now and it doesn't cost you $4.00 a month.

(The tension on the platform is gone. The plant manager goes on confidently, almost enjoying himself.)

Now, some of the things that the union *cannot* do. It cannot pay your wages or benefits, only the company can do this. The union can promise but cannot assure you of anything. They can only negotiate. Your job and my job depends, incidentally, on how well Superior negotiates. Every item you make, your company has bargained with someone on selling. A company cannot stay in business and give away more than it earns.

In closing, I would like to remind you that you do not have to vote for the union just because you have signed a card. The card places you under no obligation to the union nor can they require you to pay dues because you signed a card. In this state we have a Right-to-Work Law and you do not have to vote for the union just because you have signed a card. The card places you under no obligation to the union. The Right-to-Work Law means you do not have to belong to the union or pay dues just because someone else does. No one can lose their job because they have not joined the union or have not signed a pledge card. Don't let anyone tell you differently.

I hope, on this year, our 10th anniversary, that we can continue the same loyal interest for one another through the next 10 years as we have in these years past.

Thank you a lot.

In the election held the next day the union was soundly defeated.

The Supervisor as Crisis Communicator

The communicating doesn't end with the 25th hour speech. The daily contacts go on right up to election time. There may be a late telephone campaign by the supervisors to contact each voter, possibly to offset a last-minute issue raised by the union.

It is clear that the supervisor who is called on by his company to communicate when the union is at the gates has his problems. But he doesn't have the problem of finding something to say. The possibilities are endless. He doesn't have to question his people, spy on them, threaten them or promise them anything. These are the things that can spur trouble for the supervisor and the company.

Calmly and confidently, he can point out disadvantages of unions in general, the drawbacks of work life in the unionized company and the good things that are enjoyed under the union-free plan of operation.

Employee & Supervisor

Chapter 8
The "New" Employee

The supervisor in a union-free plant may be pardoned for thinking that turning away a union is something "they" do.

The best known actions that occur in a union campaign, and in the months and years between campaigns, are those of higher management. The captive audience speeches, the posters, the letters to workers' homes, the training of new people, the no-solicitation rules, the policy-making on unionism, handling the NLRB hearing—all are done by management at levels above the first-line supervisor.

One overriding fact, though, throws it all back into the lap of the supervisor: *The individual employee standing alone in a polling place with a ballot in his hand is the key.*

This man must be the focal point of all union-resisting activity of the supervisor and management. If a big majority can be expected to mark an "X" in the box for NO UNION on that ballot, the chances are good there will never be an election. Any alert union will discover this feeling among the employees and will search out greener pastures.

So the actions of the supervisor that count in repelling a union are those that influence the individual worker. These actions have a "fallout": profit. An employee who is disposed to mark a ballot in favor of the company will also be inclined to boost the company's ability to turn out quality products or services and to earn a profit. He will be inclined to use his imagination and talent to find better ways to do the job.

This is no magic formula, though. Merely recognizing how important the employee's feelings are, does not make them what the supervisor would like them to be.

Unions recognize the need to study the workman as the key to organizing success. Not all of their efforts have been successful, however. Solomon Barkin, then director of research of the Textile Workers of America, prepared an exhaustive "personality profile" of the union-free Southern textile worker, to help organizers in the field. Some of the highlights:

". . . The people have little experience with collective organizations; live in small towns. Their aspirations are stunted and individual initiative thwarted by a repressive folk society and the matriarchial family. They have limited alternatives and have acquiesced to the local pressures. They are avid for employment, yet fearful of the outside world and of competition from negroes. They have no strong desires for advancement . . ."

On the contrary, the experienced supervisor knows that efforts to find a "typical" worker are wasted. There is no Southern textile worker just like this profile. In fact, it appears more an excuse for the failures of the organizers than a genuine attempt to describe anyone.

The supervisor must look at his people just as they are, not as stereotypes.

A Different Worker

The employee today is not the same employee found in industry a generation ago. In the first place each individual is unique. Each individual employee, old or new, is different from anyone who has ever lived in the past or will live in the future. He is a creature of God; he has a dignified human soul.

Certainly man is the same in some ways. His body and brain have not changed significantly in the last 100,000 years. The same factors of heredity that shaped the life of the paleolithic hunter still determine a man's emotional drives, the growth and development of his body and his physiological needs. The same set of instincts acts upon his behavior.

But beyond this level of heredity and instinct, major differences can be observed between the people at work today and those of only a few decades ago. In civilized nations the age at which women reach sexual maturity has advanced more than four years in the past half century. Today's teenagers are often taller than their parents.

Experiments on laboratory animals in the first days of the animal's life show dramatic effects on its later development. The temperature and humidity of the animal's air, its nutrition, crowding and other factors have been observed to affect such traits as the animal's rate of growth, its ultimate size, its resistance to stress, its learning ability, emotional response and even behavioral patterns. It would not be too great a stretch of the imagination to believe that patterns of *human* behavior are being changed by today's environment.

The New Environment

It is widely agreed that workers today are more mobile and move more freely to new cities. But a man is also no longer a single community man. He may be born in one community, live in another, go to school in another, work in a fourth, go to church in a fifth, take recreation in others. He will often move to a new set of communities in the same area.

Home, church, school and community no longer work together to discipline and shape the individual to a common set of values. The individual may have less home life, less church life and little contact with the community, but he almost surely will have had a great deal more of an education than his predecessor in industry. He will have completed two and one half times as many years in school as the average worker of 1900 and in schools that turn out a much improved product. In earlier days the people at the lower end of the economic scale were literally out of communication with those at the upper end—that is not so today. A gap may exist, but it is not one of language and literacy.

A Labor Department survey of over 73 million workers in 1969 found their average time on the job was only 3.8 years, down 10% from just three years earlier. Average tenure of workers between 16 and 24 years old was 8½ months; over 45 was 12.7 years. Between 40 and 50 percent of non-farm workers are under 30.

The young people of today have grown up in a world community. In their time satellites have made it possible to communicate world events instantly in sight and sound and war has constantly threatened to trigger an all-out atomic blow-out.

This generation has seen amazing progress for the civil rights movement. Most supervisors have encountered this new social current on the job. There is now no minority group content to be "second class." Government duress and voluntary action by employers are rapidly making the world of work a place of truly equal opportunity.

In this connection, a further problem for supervisors is the care and handling of the formerly "hard-core" unemployed. Where many employers had practiced equal opportunity employment for years, in this "hard-core" program they give special encouragement, training and help on the job to persons who have somehow dropped out of the mainstream of the work force. This "extra opportunity" employment is new, at least on any national scale.

Even with the infusion of "hard-core" people, today's average worker, when he enters the work force, is older, has more education and is culturally mature. He has not had a background of hard work as a youth. The jobs are different mostly in their reduced physical demands, increased educational demands (many foremen of today entered industry at age 15 or younger). But the longer life enjoyed by the average workman leaves most of them working on to age 65. Work life span has increased 50% since the turn of the century. Had the starting age not risen, the work life would be almost double what it was.

Seasoned managers have observed that the "new" workers who are best qualified shy away from blue collar jobs. The heavier blue collar jobs a generation ago were occupied by a fair cross-section of the population; by people who just happened to wind up in these occupations. Today it is a group well down the initiative, responsibility and education scale. Added to this ominous trend, equal opportunity hiring has opened the doors to many who might have been thought under-qualified a few years ago. The result is a more difficult job for the supervisor. He must be a better leader and coach.

This does not tell the supervisor much he hasn't learned by experience. Describing the changes that are taking place in the work force does not help him; he has to deal with the people he has, whether or not that includes any of the new ones. If he is to create a feeling among his people of repugnance to the idea of having a union, he knows that his work is cut out for him.

This review of the facts about today's worker's background may help the supervisor see reasons for curious new attitudes. He must adapt his method of leadership to the new breed of worker coming into his work group. Most difficult of all he must understand or at least tolerate the new attitudes that this new breed brings to the workplace.

A Different Attitude

This new view of work may not be good. The semi-skilled worker today surely knows that the real work is not done by himself. It was done by some engineer who laid out the job or designed the tools. Observers see a deep problem in his loss of power and in his loss of a feeling of self-respect as a worker and of pride in his work.

Allied to this loss of pride in the job is the trend, over the years, toward less and less commitment by men and women to work, as a way of life. Paid vacations and holidays consume a larger part of the work year. It is generally assumed that the 40-hour week will not prevail through another decade. Leisure time activities occupy an ever greater part of the workers' vigor and creative talent.

This attitude toward work itself may be damaging to mental health. As one psychologist has put it:

> We don't work just to have time off from work. Work provides things leisure never can provide. Besides an income, it provides a measure of one's worth in society. It offers an identity: "I am a foreman," or "I am a salesman" are not just attempts to describe a job. In short, it provides a function in the group life that is so important to each of us. It is productive, it produces benefits both for the one who works and for others, adding meaning to life. Leisure does not do this.

In earlier days a man might have bought his own raw materials, shaped them into a useful product with his own hands, using a few simple tools and sold them at the marketplace. His success depended upon his skill. He had a sense of purpose and a feeling of accomplishment; he thought of himself as a craftsman. Many workers of today are only a couple of generations away from this man and many more are only one generation away from a family farm, where much the same brand of self-reliant life was typical. But an attitude like this is rare today.

Such a feeling could persist even in a more specialized economy, where a great part of the production cycle was under the worker's control. He could still see the results and the meaning of his work, even though his reward did not depend entirely upon his skill.

But most modern jobs make it difficult to see any meaning in work. He is alienated from any purpose in the work part of his life.

"When that five o'clock whistle blows, I nearly run to my car. I can't wait to get out of that place and I dread coming in in the morning. Putting seven bolts in the rear quarter panel of a truck day after day just isn't my idea of living. I tell my supervisor about how I feel and he reminds me of the money I'm making. I am like a vegetable."

A pessimistic observer of the work scene has said: A young man is brought up in this country to prize freedom and control of his destiny. In most jobs he is powerless, controlled by others or by a system which gives him few options.

A man's work often is without meaning because his duties seem to have no relation to his own major goals or even to the goals of the system within which he toils.

Unknown or unclear purposes of his work gives a man a feeling of not serving, of failing to function as a useful member of society and of being out of the mainstream.

Work has become a means to an end, instead of an end in itself, and that work is damaging to the man's self-esteem. The worker tends to wall his work away from his function as family man, citizen, churchman and social group member.

The supervisor can get a clearer view by sorting out the *attitudes* that are general among the "new" workers from their *reactions* to work life. The attitudes:

1. Distrust in big organizations or the establishment.
2. Increased desire for freedom, individuality, changing scene, and rapaid advancement—today.
3. Disinterest in old values—quality workmanship, responsibility, future security, busyness, strict moral code and work itself.

The reactions:

1. Will-to-work problems.
2. Little involvement with company goals.
3. Conflict between young and high-seniority employees.
4. Refusal to accept routine work as a career.
5. Drug problems at work.
6. Casual absence from work.

These reactions differ for each job. Supervisors today may remember days when these feelings and reactions on the part of workers were rare. The job often does not meet many of the needs of the workman. He needs meaning, creativity and importance in his work. This is a challenge to the supervisor.

Work a Game?

A novel idea being urged by some social scientists is that work is a game for the worker. Not the "fun" kind of game, but a set pattern of social action and counteraction. The object of the game for the individual is to protect his own self-esteem and self-image. The supervisor may be able to put this idea to use.

The theory is that the good employer must promote this sense of self-worth in the worker. Most of today's jobs tend to undermine it. Uninteresting work, socially unimportant work, meaningless (to the worker) work, unrecognized work and work in which the worker is not involved are bad games.

The worker's anti-games produce such action as absenteeism, careless workmanship, strikes, slowdowns, pilfering and personal problems. It may be observed that these anti-games are often "played" with a great deal more enthusiasm and effort than the work itself would have called for.

Symptoms of an overall no-meaning, bad game are mistrust, anxiety, aggressiveness, defensiveness, poorer communication and high vulnerability to the overtures of a labor organizer!

There are things the supervisor can do to prevent the bad games and increase the workers' sense of self-value. He can rebuild the jobs to make them fuller, more complex; enlarge the jobs to include more of the steps in the whole process; rotate employees through the various jobs in the section to prepare them for promotion and growth; and involve employees in the planning and organizing of their work when practical. Psychologist Frederick Herzberg suggests this remedy. Above all, the supervisor must bestow total respect for each of his people in all matters, both work and non-work. Psychologist and philosopher William James said, "The deepest drive in human nature is the desire to be appreciated."

The union movement feeds on the job dissatisfaction of workers. It is ironic that a union's presence in the workplace usually heightens the true dissatisfaction.

Poor Performance and Morale

Whatever the causes, the typical workman today has been described as performing at a level slightly above the minimum required to hold his job and stay on the payroll, in other words, not giving maximum energy and dedication to his work. This view is widely held.

A poll of a great many upper level executives in commerce and industry asked the question, *"Do you feel hourly paid workers in this company are a) more conscientious about their work than they were a generation ago, b) less conscientious, or c) about the same?"* Sixty-three percent thought they were less conscientious; only 2% thought they were more. Those who thought worker attitudes had worsened were asked in what ways this was shown. Less productive, slow in work, lazy, was suggested by 36%. Indifferent attitude and lack of interest was cited by 31%; and 21% said no pride in work and lower standards. Mentioned by smaller percentages were less dedication or sense of respectability, less loyalty to the company, changed to unhealthy philosophy and more supervision needed.

This scene is bad and perhaps unfair to the working man of today, but there is good reason to believe that today's workers, by and large, are less motivated. All the complaints of the executives are related to lack of motivation.

It is fair to assume that the low motivation of so many workers today results from their not getting what they want from their work. What they get is usually very much like what their supervisors and managers *think* they want.

What Do They Want?

A far-reaching survey explored the question, "Do supervisors know what their people want?" A great many supervisors were asked to rank, in the order of importance to *workers*, ten factors that are supposed to affect morale at work. The consensus of the supervisors' answers was like this:

1. Good Wages
2. Job Security
3. Promotion, growth in company
4. Good working conditions
5. Work keeping you interested
6. Personal loyalty to workers
7. Tactful disciplining
8. Full appreciation of work done
9. Sympathetic help on personal problems
10. Feeling "in" on things

Then some 35,000 workers were asked what they actually thought of these same factors. What do we see?

1. Full appreciation of work done
2. Feeling "in" on things
3. Sympathetic help on personal problems
4. Job security
5. Good wages
6. Work keeping you interested
7. Promotion, growth in company
8. Personal loyalty to workers

9. Good working conditions
10. Tactful disciplining

Unbelievably, the three lowest ranked in the supervisors' beliefs were the three highest in what the workers actually reported! What is the meaning of this? Is it "questionnaire behavior", the way a person will act when answering a questionnaire, though when given actual choices to make in real life, he will demonstrate different ideas? Probably not, because these results, or something like them, have shown up time and again in personnel research.

Motivator-Dissatisfier

A startling new idea (based on a different kind of attitude polling) may help explain this phenomenon. It is the motivator-dissatisfier theory advanced by Frederick Herzberg.

"Think of a time when you felt especially good, or especially bad, about your job—either your present job or any other job you have had—and tell me what happened." After the answer the interviewer follows up with, "How long ago did this happen? How long did the feeling last? Why did you feel the way you did? Did these feelings affect the way you did your job? How? Give me an example of the way your job was affected. Did what happened affect you personally in any way—sleep, digestion, appetite, general health? How seriously were your feelings about your job affected?"

Then, "now that you have described a time when you felt (good/bad) about your job, think of another time, one during which you felt expecially (bad/good) about your job . . ."

Herzberg took a mass of data from in-depth personal talks along these lines, classifying the kinds of events described, the duration of the feelings, how long it had been since the events had occurred, the depth of the feelings and the person's own idea of the reasons for the feeling.

An unusual pattern began to emerge. For many years the experts had accepted the idea that the effect on employees of any offering of a personnel program could be measured in a straight-line scale of bad feelings at one end and good feelings at the other. There seemed no question that each factor satisfied or dissatisfied in some proportion to the amount of it that was offered. And high satisfaction was presumed to yield high motivation. What could be more sensible?

The conclusions Herzberg drew from the facts he had gathered completely destroyed this theory. He found that those things that gave good feelings and high motivation had little power, in their absence, to dissatisfy. Removing from the scene a different set of things that dissatisfied did not seem to motivate workers. The motivators and the dissatisfiers seemed to be running on separate tracks.

The Motivators

The motivators are those factors that are closely involved with performing the work itself. Herzberg described them as,

1. *Achievement*—success in solving a problem, seeing good results of work done, completing a challenging job, having one's judgment confirmed, and the like.
2. *Recognition*—getting earned praise or esteem from superiors, subordinates, peers, the public or the company for work performance.
3. *Advancement and Growth*—getting a promotion or an upward change in status, learning a new skill.
4. *Responsibility*—being given a new key job, being allowed to work without close supervision, being accountable for one's own work or for the work of others.
5. *Work Itself*—liking one's work, doing challenging or creative work, turning out a complete piece of work.

The Dissatisfiers

The dissatisfiers turn out to be the things that have to do with the scene at work, the fringe areas of the job itself.

1. *Company Policy and Administration*—the competence of company management or organization, and the array of things we think of as personnel policies or benefit programs.
2. *Supervision-Interpersonal Relations*—relations and interaction with the supervisor and others in working hours (but not in job activities), friendships and enmities at work.
3. *Supervision-Technical*—the supervisor's ability to provide technical guidance, his competence, fairness and willingness to train.
4. *Salary*—all of the things involving compensation, fairness of the wage system, whether raises are given grudgingly or late, whether the differences in pay for different jobs are proper (absolute level of pay was seldom cited as "bad").

5. *Working Conditions*—lighting, space, ventilation, tools, shop or office location, parking space, the amount of work required (*too little work* was cited more often than too much work!).

Herzberg called these dissatisfers "hygiene" factors. They act like medical hygiene, removing health hazards from the environment, but not curing.

In studies by others along this line of thought a new dimension was added: differences were found between the levels in the chain of command and between the sexes. Thus, a lab technician feels as important motivators *responsibility* and *advancement*; technicians mention *achievement* most frequently but not as important or of such lasting duration. The dissatisfiers are *pay, supervision, company policy* and *the work itself* (though the work is normally a motivator, not a dissatisfier). Possibly the technician envies the scientists for whom he works. He does the jobs they consider beneath their dignity, so the job itself does not look so good to him. Achievement and responsibility, which make him more like the scientists, are his big boosts on the job.

The ladies, assembly workers, mention *achievement* more often than the technicians. The most important of the satisfiers, and also important dissatisfiers, were *competence of supervision* and *friendliness of supervision*. Leading the dissatisfiers were *lack of security* and *no recognition*. The anomaly here is recognition (or the absence of it) being a dissatisfier. Pay was scarcely mentioned by the women. Relations with fellow workers is important to this group.

Scientists and engineers showed results that were much alike—*achievement, recognition, advancement, responsibility*, and *the work itself* were the big positives. The two outstanding dissatisfiers were *competence of supervision* and *company policy-administration*.

Plant foremen felt as motivators *advancement, responsibility*, and more often, but less urgently, *achievement*. This reflects, perhaps, a strong need to climb up the organization ladder.

The Prescription

The message that comes through loud and clear from Herzberg is that the supervisor is wasting the company's money and kidding himself when he tries to motivate his people with larger and larger doses of the hygiene factors. These, he is saying, must be kept at adequate levels, so they don't surge up as dissatisfiers, but higher levels do not yield proportionately higher motivation.

In the morale survey cited earlier the workers are groping for "Appreciation of Work" (Recognition) and "Feeling In" or being part of the action (Responsibility). They are assigning the hygiene factors to the bottom of the heap.

Motivation is found in the things that are close to the job and job performance. It is cheaper to achieve than "hygiene" in terms of dollars but much dearer in terms of the supervisory skills that are needed. Jobs must be built to provide challenge and a chance for growth; an atmosphere of support must be maintained in which goal-setting and independent action are normal and failure is viewed as a learning tool rather than a punishable mistake.

Earned recognition and reward based on performance should be bestowed ungrudgingly. High standards should be maintained, all useful information provided, full potentials used, suggestions nurtured, training given and promotion and salary increases tied to merit. These are the signs that the supervisor is taking Herzberg's suggestions for a higher performance.

This theory and the prescription are being widely accepted in industry. But in the workplace which has, and should hold on to, a union-free status, there is danger in stressing the "motivators" too much. A union will usually attack through the "dissatisfiers."

The union organizer thrives on dissatisfaction. This is his particular area of competence, promoting unrest and using it to his own advantage. The pieces in his game are the items that can be described and manipulated: pay rates, benefit plans, hours of work, distribution of overtime, unfair treatment, unfriendly supervision, etc. These are all dissatisfiers. The supervisor of the union-free group must not be hypnotized by the peak performance and profit that can come from high motivation. Building it is a long process and he can lose it all to the built-in inefficiencies of unionism by allowing the dissatisfiers to grow.

In short, the supervisor who would help his company remain union-free cannot afford to give total commitment to the motivators. The hygiene factors can kill him.

The Group

Sam Huff, reflecting on the adjustment from linebacker on the All-Pro football team to salesman for a textile manufacturer: ". . . everybody knows the part about being cheered, having your name in the papers, being recognized on the street . . . I miss most *the something special about being part of a team of guys who all speak the same language and who appreciate what you're doing.*"

Compounding the problems of coping with the "new" employee, as any experienced supervisor will point out, employees don't come one by one; in bunches they do not act the same as any one of them taken individually.

The work group itself has a life of its own. A worker's attitudes are always being shaped by the pressures of this and other groups of which he is a member. He is a member of a family group; a citizen of the nation, state, city and school district; a neighbor in a neighborhood; and he is a member, possibly, of a great variety of voluntary associations—a church, a bowling team, bridge club, civic organization or social group.

The point that the supervisor must not forget is that the work group by no means takes up all of the worker's "group" time. The group at work will often be of rather low importance to him and may have but little influence on his behavior.

Companies often depend on the employee's outside groups to help influence his decision on unionism. For example, looking at the individual alone might lead to handling all "vote *NO UNION*" letters direct to him at work. But it has been observed that the mailing piece to the home (the notorious "Dear Mary and John" letter) is one of the most effective communications. There it will be read and absorbed by his family. Their influence will bear on him.

Similarly, group influences may lead the company to channel a certain idea through a person or group in the community, rather than through company sources. Local bankers or a business development committee may be convinced that union advances in the community will hurt the influx of new industry. The management cannot bring this message to the workers effectively, but one of the outside sources surely can.

The supervisor can establish better rapport with his people at work by outside group associations. Such contacts can produce clear insights into the workers' feelings.

The man in a group is a different man. He craves the group's respect and wants to belong so badly that he will conveniently stretch his own judgment and put off his own desires to be in agreement with the group. A researcher in group psychology showed how strong these feelings can be:

Working with groups of people only casually acquainted, the researcher arranged it so that all but one of each group were "in," cooperating in the experiment. He would give the group simple judgments to make, such as deciding which of two circles on the blackboard were larger, then have each one say which one he thought it was. After a few times around the group for decisions of this sort, by prearrangement he would have each one in the group give an obviously wrong decision before it was the "subject's" turn to answer. What do you suppose happened? In all cases the subject was clearly under great strain and in one of three cases he gave the wrong answer!

In a group a person will accept suggestions more readily; ideas are not closely examined but are readily accepted as true. "Catch words" or slogans serve to communicate.

Individuals will do things in groups they would never do alone. Lynchings, mob violence and strike violence are examples. These are extreme situations, but on a lesser scale a person can be changed by the common work group and the other groups to which he belongs.

In the work situation the work group shares many things in common (including a supervisor) so that the interests of the individual and the group are very close. It has an informal code of conduct. Its members are aware of one another. When one member of the group has a good thing happen to him at work, the whole group gets a lift. Likewise, a reverse for one is a reverse for all. The old rule, "Criticize in private, praise in public," is not followed just for its effect on the individual, but for the equally important effect on his group.

Union organizers do not hesitate to take advantage of group phenomena. A handbook for organizers states:

> The night before the election is the big night. Every effort should be made to have maximum attendance at this meeting. If necessary, door prizes should be given. The meeting should be kept an enthusiastic one. Use rank and file members as much as possible. They should tell why they are voting for the union. Don't leave any of the employer's arguments unanswered. Pass out sample ballots and have each one vote. Count the ballots and announce the vote . . .

So the supervisor, among his other talents, has to be a practical group psychologist. He must have a "feel" for how his actions and words will be received in the group. He must identify the natural leaders within his work group, singling them out for special attention to build good attitudes. He will clear new ideas with them in advance in certain situations, where acceptance would be doubtful if the whole group were approached "cold."

The employee nears his full potential when he is a contributing member of a work team that has high performance goals, good ability to interact and high group pride and loyalty. He is near his potential both in productivity and in job satisfaction.

The New Breed

Leading the worker of today, with all his new attitudes, demands new skills. But more urgently, it demands new leader attitudes.

The union-free supervisor will keep his thoughts on the individual employee standing alone in a voting booth, ballot in hand. Some will be of the new breed, some of them of the old school, but surely each of them will be a proud individual. Each will respond to the leader who recognizes his need for a satisfying job, who gives him a place for work that is reasonably free of dissatisfiers and who accepts the proposition that the work group has its own personality.

Is the "new breed" more apt to embrace unionism? On the record to date the answer is *no*. He may be more inclined to oppose "the establishment", but the union quite often represents an "establishment" to him. Whatever the reason, rather than have a union deal for him, he is apt to prefer face-to-face dealing with his employer and all the personal freedoms that go with the union-free workplace.

The supervisor can see that his part in this picture is as a possible dissatisfier. Union organizers seize upon unpopular and alleged unfair supervisors as the best kind of campaign ammunition. But this only begins the supervisor's responsibility. He is involved with all of the factors that the motivator-dissatisfier theory sees as important. The other dissatisfiers. The motivators. The whole scene.

The new workman cannot be summarized or capsulized; each one is unique. It would be accurate to say that even the lowest employee on the social scale, in education or in intelligence, deserves the total respect of his supervisor. This is no short cut to persuasion. There are few things that can be said or actions taken that will influence all employees in the same way.

Today the work scene is different. The workers seem to have changed. But leadership is still person-to-person.

Chapter 9

The New Supervision
Fresh Goals and Skills

A growing body of opinion holds that the best industrial relations department is the least industrial relations department.

Experts believe it is the man responsible for the amount and quality of production, not a group of personnel specialists, who is best able to reward, discipline, lead and motivate the workers. In the larger companies now, more of the functions of "personnel" people are being shifted to the first line supervisor. It has always been this way in the smaller companies.

So the first line supervisor or foreman is a key man. His new functions clearly call for new skills that must be mastered. He finds himself in the middle. Most supervisors are technically competent (they are usually chosen on that basis), but they have learned that technical competence is only one side of the job. He is also an administrator, a coach and a leader.

In a single day's work he may be an observer, a doer, an appraiser, a follower, an advisor, a resource person, a gadfly, an arbitrator, a change agent and a liaison man. Some will boggle at the task and turn in a poor job by doing only the part of it they can do easily. Some have the hangup that they are not given enough freedom and power in their jobs. The successful supervisor will have a wholesome attitude about his job and will accept it as it is.

The Importance of Attitude

The supervisor's attitude should be, first, that the company is not something that is there, like Everest. There is a feeling abroad that to be in business is to be rich; for a corporation, to exist is to succeed. Nothing could be further from the truth.

It is like saying that frontier marshal Wyatt Earp never lost a gun battle because so many songs and stories were written about him. It seems obvious that it is the other way around: the songs and stories appeared because he was never runner-up in a shoot-out.

It is seldom easy to sort out cause and effect in economics, but it should not be hard to understand that the great number of successful corporations are not successful because they exist, but, rather, exist because they are successful. Neither are they successful because they are big; they are big because they are successful.

Similar to the idea that success is sure, there sometimes is a vague feeling that "business" is bad and there is something to be ashamed of in working for a company. A cold look at this idea tells us that a corporation is just one of many kinds of organizations that are important in our lives, even more important in our lives than most of the others. Our business system is the way the nation makes a living for itself; it is the fountainhead of true national wealth and power. Our system is the most effective in the world. The corporation is not a thing to be ashamed of. And the effective supervisor feels that he is a part of this.

Another attitude of the effective first-line supervisor is openness to self-improvement. He can find plenty of advice. Endless articles, seminars and books are available to help him in the many sides of his job. But much of the advice frustrates him. In the first place, the "mix" of duties is rarely the same for any two supervisors' jobs or, for that matter, for two people who fill what should be the same job (according to a job description).

He will read advice telling him to do things which he has no authority to do. Authority levels, when a decision is needed, might be described as follows:

1. Makes decision on own; takes action.
2. Makes decision, takes action and informs boss.
3. Talks to boss before deciding, but decides.
4. Recommends a decision to higher authority.
5. Leaves decision to others.

This is not to say that any supervisor will fit neatly into one of the slots. Much depends on the kind of action to be taken or the decision that is to be made. For instance, the final decision to discharge an employee is often withheld from the first-line supervisor, though he will nearly always have the authority to suspend an employee while his recommendation to discharge him is being reviewed by higher-ups. This is Level *1* and Level *4* above.

Most supervisors will have Level *1* authority in assignment of people to get the job done. Promotions within his group will usually be at Level *3*. There is no uniformity, even within companies, however.

Other things reduce the supervisor's freedom of action: higher management's demands on him, "staff" specialists' suggestions, paperwork, law requirements, other supervisors' demands, etc. He sometimes feels he can no longer promote deserving men, adjust wage inequities, develop better machines and methods, transfer or discharge people or even plan the work of his department on his own, much less stay alert to the needs and wants of the people he supervises.

It is hard for the first-line supervisor to be the leader that modern managers expect him to be. From above he seems to hear he should be an overseer, not a leader. The easy way out is to retreat and complain about his lack of true authority. The real challenge to the supervisor today is to accept the ground rules and move on to assert the leadership and the personal touch that is needed. Nearly all supervisors have the same problems.

Self Improvement

No one thing can be said here that will help all supervisors. Their problems are so diverse that even the most general ideas will not touch everyone. But a pattern emerges when we look at the content of supervisor training courses and note the opinions of the people who have studied supervisors at work. Some important areas to look are a) the areas of skill and what he should be doing; b) what a supervisor should be, his traits and abilities; c) the problem areas of the supervisor's job; d) how to do it, along with some of the theories of supervisory style, leadership and charisma; and e) the new role of the supervisor today.

Most of the points we will see are people-oriented. This analysis does not take full account of the fact that in most cases a supervisor must be a competent worker. He is on a hopeless spot when his people think he doesn't know enough about the work, or any work of the company (a workman is apt to recognize competence in other areas, and make allowances for things the boss doesn't know about his particular job or project).

We have seen that the supervisor is a jack-of-all-trades, including technical man, businessman, administrator, coach and, above all, leader. Still, most of the advice a supervisor finds in print is centered on the last two. Perhaps this is because technical ability and administration skill are tied so closely to particular jobs and actual company situations. Teaching these is considered more in the nature of orientation than general development. Or perhaps his skill here is not questioned.

Areas of Skill

Training Factors

A look at a few curricula of supervisor training courses gives us a good overall view of the areas that are thought important, or at least teachable, in the supervisor's job.

One course will include:

1. Making the move up to the foreman job.
2. Management tools: planning, setting goals, organizing for results, delegating, supervising, follow-through and control.
3. Problem-solving: getting the facts, evaluating the situation, human considerations, developing alternative courses of action, weighing pros and cons, risk and action.
4. Managing people: techniques, communicating, dealing with grievances and discipline, training and developing employees, human relations and motivation.
5. Achieving efficient operations.
6. Cultivating a positive job attitude and identifying with management goals.
7. Self-development.

Another course will list:

1. Scope of the job: planning, organizing, directing, controlling and appraising.
2. Motivation and direction of people.
3. Communication.
4. Planning and assigning work.
5. Cost reduction.
6. Manufacturing controls.
7. Labor relations.

A third program will feature:

1. The supervisor's role: supervision styles, assumptions about people, etc.

2. Planning, scheduling and controlling: goal setting, time study, risk, PERT, work standards, sampling and evaluating work.

3. Training and developing others.

4. Work simplification.

5. Evaluating employees.

6. Face-to-face communication: aim, bias and climate, questioning and probing.

7. Human relations: human needs and organizational goals, job satisfaction, self-fulfillment, status and role, achievement and affiliation and power needs.

8. Listening—barriers.

9. Writing: Clarity, completeness, conciseness, character and courtesy.

10. Developing insight and sensitivity: role playing and leading a discussion.

These topics provide the supervisor with a good idea of the skills that training experts believe every good supervisor should have.

Appraisal Factors

To find a consensus of informed opinion on the key areas of supervisory skill, we must consider more than the training that is offered. We must also look at the factors of performance upon which the supervisor is judged—appraisal check points. Three typical lists of factors used to appraise supervisory ability are summarized below:

List One

1. Planning: Uses own time and the time of others well? Goals and priorities set? Equipment and materials available? Uses employee skills wisely?

2. Organization: Do his people know what is expected? Defines responsibilities clearly?

3. Delegation: Passes responsibility and authority down the line?

4. Work relationships (outside of own group): Cooperates? Supports policy and established procedure?

5. Control-coordination: Coordinates well with other departments? Meets performance requirements? Controls cost?

6. Development of People: Orients people effectively? Encourages subordinates to develop? Has replacements ready? Picks the right men for the job? Continues self-improvement?

7. Communication: Keeps people informed? Writes and speaks clearly? Listens well? Invites criticism, other upward communication?

8. Human Relations: Sensitive to his people's needs? Tolerates differences?

9. Innovation, Initiative: Sees where change is needed? Responds to new ideas? Accepts suggestions? Encourages creative thinking?

List Two

Rate his competence in:

1. Order giving
2. Training employees
3. Appraising employee performance
4. Preventing and handling grievances
5. Making decisions
6. Initiating changes

List Three

How good is he in:

1. Keeping his employees informed (of what they need to know of what is going on).

2. Allowing his employees to influence supervisor (on decisions where their experience and knowledge should carry weight).

3. Allowing and encouraging his employees to make decisions.

4. Encouraging his employees to work hard and to do high quality work.

5. Giving guidance and assistance to his employees.

6. Communicating and getting acceptance for the objectives of his part of the organization.

7. Avoiding waste and unnecessary work—wise use of money and manpower.

8. Judging and appraising employee performance.

9. Selecting most capable employees.

10. Achieving teamwork among employees.

11. Delegating necessary authority.

The training topics and the appraisal areas reflect the key acts the supervisor is expected to master. He should not wait for his employer to improve his areas of weakness. He should continually try to develop himself.

What He Should Be

A common approach to developing or finding better supervisors is defining the traits of the effective supervisor. This is not particularly helpful to the supervisor who wants to improve himself, since traits are not subject to great changes. But to the extent that a man can consciously modify his own behavior, perhaps project a different image, a review of the good traits may be of use. Certainly the supervisor can identify the traits in which he is strong and build on them.

The traits usually mentioned by managers are not those that have to do with technical ability. They are mostly concerned with the supervisor's relationships with his people. A careful listing of desirable supervisor traits yields these attributes:

Self-assured and confident.

Able to talk to workers regarding their problems and to give effective orders, instruction and training.

Cooperative and able to get the cooperation of others.

Generates enthusiasm.

Understands people and their needs.

Safety-minded.

Feels himself a representative of management and, at the same time, a representative of the people he leads.

Personally efficient in the use of time and considerate of the time of others.

Open to the ideas of others, particularly those whom he supervises.

Interested in each one of his people as a person.

Helps his people satisfy their desires for security, recognition and opportunity in the job.

Firm but fair.

Leads without exercise of bare authority.

Admits his own mistakes.

Truthful, particularly regarding job performance of his people (constant urging to pour on credit and praise leads many supervisors to stretch the truth. The chickens will come home to roost).

Consistent, not moody, in actions and attitude (A predictable supervisor is a source of great security to an employee).

A self-starter. Doesn't wait for the whip to crack, but stays on top of new ideas and approaches as a way of life.

Reads and learns and takes advantage of every training opportunity available to him.

The managers appear to take it for granted that the supervisor is technically qualified, works hard and is personally involved with achieving high quality output at low cost.

The Problem Areas

A great problem facing the supervisor today is the onset of new knowledge. To do his job he may have to cope with mathematical modeling, linear programming, statistical quality control and tools that are, in many cases, out of his grasp. He finds himself surrendering his authority to staff people who have command of these new methods. He must find ways to adapt and keep control, because the chances are that the new systems can't get off the ground without him.

Most serious of the problems affecting supervisors, though, is unwillingness to do the things they know they should do. It is like the farmer who declines to buy the book on new concepts in agriculture because he knows he is not farming as well as he knows how to farm now.

For example, all supervisors know that good communication is needed. But a well-documented survey which focused on dissatisfied workers found that their supervisors were communicating very poorly.

Only a few workers felt their supervisors had fully explained to them company policies and operations. No more than one third felt their foremen ever gave them a chance to explain their own ideas and a third felt their foremen would get angry if conversation touched on sensitive areas. They said they get most of their information from the grapevine.

Ninety percent reported their supervisors used only one method of communication. Many reported actual defects of speech.

In the matter of "support" (a broad term that refers to the supervisory atmosphere of the job, whether people are encouraged, defended against outside criticism and given help to grow) only one fourth of these workers thought they worked in a supportive atmosphere.

Regarding explanations and instructions, nearly half found fault, calling the supervisor's words vague, confusing and contradictory. A whopping eighty percent thought their supervisors *would rather discharge them than give constructive suggestions* to improve low performance. In this same vein a substantial number reported veiled threats and derogatory remarks by their supervisors.

These are opinions of dissatisfied workers. Faulty communication by supervisors has helped put them in the ranks of the dissatisfied. The area of communications is at the heart of human relations. Human relations is, after all, the supervisor's dealings with his people; it is the words he uses, the tone of his voice, his gestures, facial expressions, even his silences, as much as it is his official acts.

Supervisor delinquency has been summed up in the "Six Sins".

1. *Being a boss rather than a leader*—it seems much easier to handle problems if he doesn't have to consider operating suggestions by his people and possible errors in the way he has lined out the work.

2. *Failure to make himself clear*—instructions to simply "get going on this problem" don't give the guidance needed or, more important, the power a subordinate may need. The jobs in the department will swell and shrink according to the individual ambition and power hunger of the employees.

3. *Snap judgment in the selection of employees*—a foreman who selects a new worker by a gut feeling that he is the right kind will have years of frustration to show for his hasty choice.

4. *Too busy to train*—sometimes it takes time to save time and time spent training is one of those times. Output is only briefly increased by pressure tactics. The way for a supervisor to get lasting productivity is by sound training and planned growth of his people.

5. *Playing things "close to the vest"*—nobody knows where this foreman stands. He keeps it all to himself. He may think his people are not interested, he may be fearful the information he has is not complete and may be misleading, but he will find overloads, slowdowns, missed goals and turnover rising to meet him.

6. *Indifference to recognition and discipline*—the supervisor who drags his feet in recognizing the good performer and disciplining the misbehaver destroys morale. He must require acceptable work and he must recognize and reward, in some way, superior achievement.

As if the cards were not already stacked against the leader, the behavioral scientists are finding now that the response of individuals to a particular action by the supervisor cannot be predicted. A person's own perception of his past experience and his environment cannot be understood by a supervisor. A good example of this, that most supervisors have noted, is the effect of discipline on a worker. To some it will be a motivator; to others it may cause an opposite reaction, the mental "quit".

But even the supervisor who does what he is supposed to do and is what he is supposed to be, may yet have his problems. He may not be in proper "style".

Style

"Leadership Style" describes a quality that is more than behavior; it is the leader's general approach to his task of getting work done by his group. One expert has defined leadership style as activity that meets the deep personal needs of the supervisor in his work. It is not the specific acts; it is the way he goes about them.

Most popular of the recent writings about leadership style is the "management grid" idea that a leader can be placed at a fairly precise point on a chart by plotting his position on two scales: a) the degree to which he emphasizes output and b) the degree of his concern for human values. These values are determined by thorough testing. Scales are numbered one through nine and the game is to move each leader toward the coveted 9,9 position (great concern for output plus great concern for human values) by development activities.

The 9,1 supervisor sees his job as meeting schedules, getting production out, and telling people what to do. The 1,9 man is for a "country club" air; a happy and contented work force even though production suffers. He has a concern for output, but not to the extent of "pressuring" people. At 9,9 we see a team manager, or better, a coach who makes decisions and gives leadership, but is not the whole team. He assumes there is no important conflict between personal and company goals.

This is not to belittle the management grid as some sort of pointless game of chess moves from 1,1 to 9,9. It is more a system of management and management training. Once a foreman has found his place on the grid he has a roadmap to the personal and organizational changes needed to improve himself and the work climate. Training is given, first to develop openness and teamwork within groups of managers, followed up with later phases of training that give rise to changes in the organization itself.

One company has used a similar chart based on concern for organizational goals and concern for human needs. At the highest in both, the supervisor is termed "Manager"; high in human needs but low in organizational goals, he is called "Missionary"; and at the top of the organization goal pole he was an "Autocrat". In the middle he was "Compromiser" and low scores in both categories are termed

"Deserters". The charting is used to fix the content of training to be given the supervisor.

Another approach to pinning down "leadership style" works with two pairs of opposites: hostile-warm (friendly); and submissive-dominant. The supervisor classifies himself by his reaction to a series of statements such as: "You seldom argue with your boss," "You prefer tact and diplomacy to forthrightness," and "You are a take-charge kind of guy." "Off the job you have more friends than most people in your group." "You get along well with your fellow managers." "You resent people who get in your way, preventing you from achieving your objectives." He can then locate his scores on crossing axis lines, each representing the paired opposites, and mark them. Connecting the points he finds a line of distinctive angle and length, relative to the four quadrangles: submissive-hostile, submissive-friendly, dominant-friendly and dominant-hostile.

No point is made of one position being better than another, only that the supervisor see that a certain kind of leadership is natural to him. The improvement is up to him. He may wish to work to improve an image he is projecting or to build up a strong point. A supervisor who finds himself in the submissive-friendly quarter, for example, should think about using a more participative and democratic method of leading.

On a different course is the consideration-structure approach to style. *Consideration* is the concern for establishing mutual respect and trust and a warm rapport, not just the "pat on the back" kind of good relations, but a real concern for meeting employee needs. *Structure* is the extent to which a supervisor organizes and specifies his group's action and how he defines his relationship with the group. For example, it is a structure "high" if he assigns each member to a role, assigns tasks, decides how to do things, pushes for production and clearly supports organizational goals.

These do not appear to operate within the supervisor as opposites, one or the other, but can exist side by side. There is no best answer. Every job would seem to require a slightly different mixture of the two factors for ideal results. It is the supervisor's task to decide the changes he might effect in his style to perform better in each part of his job.

Leaders are Made, Not Born

Studies indicate that almost anyone who aspires to become a leader can become one with work and study, but he must be aware that certain work situations will not fit his style of leading. Changing leadership style can be a great mistake. Leadership style is an expression of personality, and big changes here are not practical.

One problem is that he may see himself as an open and fair supervisor whom his people respect and admire. They in fact perceive him as a cold-hearted autocrat who isn't really concerned for them as human beings. A supervisor doesn't usually give much thought to his leadership style and he usually holds a distorted view of his own image with his people. He may actually be concerned for them, but has no acceptable way to express it. Just knowing this will help. Cold self-study is needed.

The leader should learn to recognize those situations where his style is apt to fail and avoid them if possible. He should try to make the situation fit his style, but just knowing where the danger points lie will go a long way toward making him a better supervisor.

So *style* in leadership is, according to the experts, not a matter of introvert vs. extrovert, aggressive vs. submissive, loudness vs. quietness, devil-may-care vs. cautious, or kind vs. mean. It is mostly the mix between getting out the work and getting along with people. Not that both can't be done, but there appears to be one best mixture of the elements for each job situation.

How It's Done

Though he knows he cannot change what he is, the successful supervisor will zero in on the things he should be doing and will look for ways to do his job better and to build on his personal supervisory style.

What does he do to improve? He can be aware of what he should be doing, of what he should be in the eyes of his men and of the various styles of leadership. There remain a few specifics that are widely accepted. Again, leave aside that part of his job that requires the supervisor, in spite of all kinds of outside pressures, to meet the schedule, keep costs down, reduce defects of bad service, keep required records, submit reports and maintain a good safety record. Look at the part of the job that requires him to maintain a smooth-running, efficient work team, at best a happy and harmonious group but at least a group that has no profit-eroding personal upsets.

Man Study is the first step for a supervisor in building the kind of relationships and rapport he needs.

Excerpt From an Interview
with a Successful Japanese Industrialist

"You have the reputation of being a great judge of men. How do you pick them?"

"As a matter of fact, it is extremely difficult to judge men. In my opinion, one can be only 60 percent effective in judging people. If I become confident of 60 percent of their capability, I let them do as they wish and see what they will come up with. Fortunately, this system has resulted in relatively few mistakes."

The supervisor must know what is on the record about the background of each of his people. Then, through conversation or casual interview he must learn what is between the lines of the record—his home life, his family, his standing in his community, his religious and moral beliefs, what he does for amusement, his hobbies, what he needs from his work and what his ambitions are. On the job is he an "idea man" or creator? Is he one of those people who always seems to get the job done, no matter how difficult? (Or the reverse or somewhere in between?) What part of the job does he do best? Can he do only a part of the job well? Is he a follower or is he one of the natural leaders?

This knowledge must not be kept on the shelf. It is used in tapping the man's full potential, in building closer relations.

The next question put to the Japanese industrialist was:
'One of your maxims is, 'Ordinary people can be trained and developed to do extraordinary work.' Can you elaborate on that?"

"It is very hard for anybody to achieve anything without constant and conscious effort. But the important thing is that everyone has a unique, natural gift. We must make every effort to develop the gift. Sometimes this is easier to do than at other times."

The supervisor's *man study* goes on to study the individual as a part of the work group: the patterns of friendship, the cliques, the "pecking order" or status position of each one in the group, the accepted leaders, the informer, the clown and the messenger. Again the knowledge must not be wasted. It is used in building an effective team by keeping enemies apart, by using friends on sub-teams, rotating people often enough to avoid forming cliques, (as opposed to teams) in work sub-groups.

Man study most of all involves empathy—the ability to put oneself into the other man's shoes, and feel what he feels. It cannot be done from a distance, but only down in the trenches and in a deliberate way.

Pointers on Leadership. Business literature is full of pointers on leadership. Some of the key situations are:

1. *Giving Instructions and Orders.* The supervisor must come straight to the point. He must convey the *why* of the instructions, unless it is obvious. He must make his meaning plain and leave no doubts, uncertainty or feelings of inadequacy.

2. *Building Job Understanding.* The supervisor must be sure each one knows what his job is, whom he must work with, what it is to do well on the job and how well he is doing the job. How his job is important to the success of the company and why the company needs to meet competition through changes and improvement in methods, machinery and job assignment.

3. *Dealing with Employee Complaints.* Anticipation and prevention are the best medicine, but whether the complaint is based on fact or is without merit, the supervisor must assume that it is a very real and important issue in the eyes of the worker. The best thinking today says that employees should be encouraged to discuss their complaints. The good supervisor is not necessarily the one who has the fewest complaints, but more likely the one to whom the most are brought.

4. *Recognizing Unhealthy Situations.* The supervisor must be alert to signs of mistrust, hostility, discontent, and tension in his own department and in others. He must be willing to bring such findings to the attention of higher management.

5. *Dealing with Day-to-day Routine.* The supervisor must be sure his people can rely on his fair play, his consistency, his acting only on the facts, his willingness to delegate and not over-supervise. He must keep his eye on the main chance, the real goals. He should give recognition when it is due and promote involvement by keeping his people "in the know", by allowing them to help in the planning wherever possible and by seeking their counsel in decisions, if their ideas can help.

Giving Work New Meaning. One facet of leadership that many a supervisor has not faced up to is giving work new meaning. This is the effort to structure jobs to make them interesting, then to select and place his people in these jobs according to their talents and to give them a sense of purpose and proprietorship. The supervisor must regularly review the content of each job from the employee's point of view. He should study especially the jobs where high turnover occurs. Are the tasks creative, demanding, useful, or routine and limited? He should consider injecting variety by putting several repetitive tasks together in one assignment. In some jobs it may be possible to add the inspection function to the individual task of production, making the man responsible for the quality of his own output.

The Exit Interview

"Do you think you received enough recognition for the work you were doing?"

"Recognition? For that dumb job?"

The young Personnel Assistant, trying to recall something from his studies toward his bachelors degree in psychology that would help him in this situation, switches the approach: "What did you like best about working here?" (good question: limited possibilities, all of them good!)

"The pay."

"Well, what did you like the least?" (Not too much of a mistake—maybe he will hold it down to one or two things).

"The pay."

The Personnel Assistant is clearly rattled: "Look, how can you like the pay the best *and* the least?"

"It was good enough to keep me on this dumb job!"

People can develop a sense of purpose in their work when they are able to see the connection between what they do and the finished product or service. The supervisor should appeal to their feeling of ownership or territory by referring to *your* job, *your* machine or *your* report. To the group he should talk of *our* unit, *our* group, *our* job or *our* company.

A supervisor may regard the actual work as just routine and think people are motivated by things that please them in a personal or physical way, such as fringe benefits, lighting, air conditioning or a good social climate. Not so. To find the root causes of poor workmanship, high employee turnover, strikes and attempted union organizing, fatigue and resentment, a study was made of eight job-related factors:

1. Responsibility for own work—extent to which worker can use his own discretion.
2. Hours—the shift change times.
3. Repetitiveness of the work.
4. Physical activity—is the work sedentary or is great physical energy required? Able to move about?
5. Rotation between work stations.
6. Goals—eventual use of the product; amount of production.

7. Group Effects—individual task, or small groups? Small groups working in cooperation?

8. Use of training in the importance of the job, personal investment in the work.

Confirming the theorists, the study determined that the work should not be routine and that the workmen are motivated as a) they succeed in, and are recognized for, their work; b) they advance in responsibility, skill and knowledge; c) the work seems important to them and they are emotionally involved with its success. The foreman, it was shown, should look for opportunities for the workmen to exercise their own judgment, to help in the design of the job and in establishing work methods and performance goals. He should show them how their jobs fit into the entire business. The study suggested creating sub-goals to measure accomplishment in those jobs where workers cannot see the finished product.

Some of the findings were unusual. The study suggested that employees should know regularly how they are doing; not just recognition for good work, but also notification of errors. Occasional physical activity—walking about, changing position—seems linked with higher motivation. Regular rotation on job stations is linked with higher motivation, but rotating only occasionally seemed to kill motivation.

Perhaps the most important of the factors was the responsibility of the worker and the discretion he is allowed at work. High responsibility yielded high motivation and pride in the work.

A caution: the supervisor must often be a salesman to introduce enriched jobs. He must be sure his people do not think it is some kind of "speed-up" or "stretch-out". And if he is acting on his own, he may face a selling job to convince his own management of its effectiveness.

Discipline

By definition, discipline is training which corrects, molds, strengthens or perfects; control gained by enforcing obedience, order, or punishment and chastisement. In industry the word discipline calls to mind the last definition. But punishment is not the best way to induce good behavior. This teaches employees what not to do. More particularly, they are being shown what they should not have done, not what to do in the future. Punishment puts the emphasis on being caught, rather than doing right.

Leniency is equally ineffective. The supervisor appears to condone breaking the rules but then may over-react when a number of minor infractions have been committed and his breaking point is reached.

Self-Policing Discipline

New ideas are turning up in discipline. Most promising is the self-policing method mentioned in Chapter 3. In this approach the assumption is made that the employee is not in grade school and teacher isn't going to slap his wrist for rule infractions. He is considered responsible for his own behavior.

A first infraction is met by a notification of the infraction and a reminder to the worker of his responsibility. Of course deliberate, major infractions are not handled this way. There will always be actions—fighting on the job, drunkenness at work, criminality at work—which must be met with suspension and often discharge. In the self-policing method a series of steps are taken if offenses continue. The number of steps varies in various plans, but at each step more intensive attention and counseling is given. Higher management is involved in the last stages and the employee is made responsible for deciding whether he intends to meet the company's standards. If he is determined to stay he must propose what he intends to do to keep his behavior in line. In effect, he sets behavior goals for himself. In practice the employee will often resign his position. Terminating a man's services is the final step that only occurs when it is clear that he cannot correct his behavior and he is unsuitable for the job.

Needless to say, this approach to discipline is totally unusable in a unionized plant. A supervisor may not use it in his own department, unless it is to be used alike by all departments.

Communicating Discipline

In criticizing, reproaching or informing employees of missteps under the self-policing method the good supervisor will be careful to choose the proper time and place, will focus on the act and will be very specific about the act and the remedy.

A man will often admit his error and take instruction, but seldom will he do so before an audience. This type of discussion should be private. Timing is important, though there are no set rules. It is a matter of judgment. Conventional wisdom has it that shortly before lunch time is not good because of its effects on digestion and that end-of-the-day sessions are poor because of the possibility that a discussion will be cut short or hurried. A time early in the morning, allowing time later in the day for further, friendly, contact is considered best for most purposes.

In a discipline discussion, the talk should be about the happening and the situation. The point is to keep the person out of it. It may be well to point out to the man that others have made the same mistake and they have corrected their errors and he can too. Generalities about conduct are unacceptable. Exaggerations are equally bad. These cause him to ignore your valid criticism and he will resist correction.

There is a true art to telling another person he is wrong. A supervisor's instinct is to get angry and let it be known. This will usually cause the person to heat up. An unpleasant situation is the result. But on the other hand, there is an element of phoniness in pretending to be undisturbed.

A new approach to this has the offended supervisor expressing his own feelings to the offender, all the while staying as calm as possible. For example, a two-day project is almost completed but the results are substantially nullified because of the failure of a subordinate to follow instructions. The instinctive reaction is like, "How could you make such a stupid mistake?" Considered much better is, "I feel angry and totally frustrated because of all the time we have wasted." Openly sharing feelings, and the reasons for them, yields plusses in situations other than disciplinary discussions. However, it is a better idea to personalize good feelings by praise for the person, rather than the roundabout way of stating one's own feelings of pleasure and the reason for them.

Consistent discipline is necessary to maintain high morale. People have a real need for correction and guidance in order to be successful in their work. The supervisor should search his own motives to be sure he is not dealing out discipline to harass an employee he doesn't like, or is getting tough mainly to satisfy his own ego.

Charisma

Most supervisors would like to have more "charisma", that quality in a person that causes others to follow him. With some it seems to be inborn. Psychologists reject this idea, however, believing that such cases are due to early environment rather than to any hereditary trait. Logically, charisma results from actions of the leader as perceived by his followers. It would seem that something could be done about gaining or building charisma.

To do this ask yourself what kind of leader you respond to at work. Most respond to the leader who represents a way to satisfy needs for recognition, for responsibility, for advancement, for reassurance, for challenging work, for support and for more compensation. We constantly judge the man under whom we serve in terms of what he can do for us. Now turn this around and ask if you are doing this for your people.

A second observation about charisma is that it is seldom possessed by people who are lethargic and uncommitted. Charismatic leaders tend to be hard-working, totally dedicated people and they act out their dedication to the goals at hand. A leader cannot motivate others without being himself motivated. His mind and the values that he holds and shows each day must be such that his people will want to follow him. The supervisor should ask himself, "Could I still lead on the job if I had no rank? Is the quality of my example adequate?"

In industry, charisma is not the charisma of history, although there are resemblances. The political charismatic person relies on persuasion power to dominate rather than on some outside authority. His tools are a mixture of the use of language, logic, emotion and personality. Typically, also, his charisma is short-lived or is at least unstable. This kind of leader has to keep supplying miracles if he is to maintain control. He must believe absolutely that he has the answers to the problems at hand; he must believe in himself as the one person who can solve the problem; and he must be an effective communicator.

In industry, the same qualities, when not carried to such extremes, are exactly those that make the outstanding leader—self-confidence, energy, dedication, the ability to communicate, a good sense of the practical and a willingness to take reasonable risks.

The Types of Leadership

Not precisely the "leadership style", which we have examined, are the methods of leadership:

1. *Autocratic leadership*—the one-man operation of determining policy and making decisions and seeking obedience from the group.
2. *Democratic Leadership*—encouraging the group to take part in setting policies and originating ideas.
3. *Laissez-faire Leadership*—that method in which the leader does not take an important part in the group's specific activity, but acts more as an information center.

The three methods are not mutually exclusive. A good leader will exercise all three at times, selectively. He may direct a subordinate to pick up an order (autocratic); he may consult with his people on the best way to set about accomplishing a project (democratic); and he may leave them completely alone when they are on the right track (laissez-faire). Though one recognizes that his leadership style is not subject to great change, he should not surrender the idea of using different methods and different approaches to supervising.

The "New" Supervisor

Is the job of supervising today any different than it has always been? Perhaps not, but there seem to be distinct changes taking place. There is much more emphasis now on the supervisor's re-building jobs and bringing out the potential abilities of his people. The latest thinking on motivation indicates that the supervisor himself is not important as a motivating factor. He was seldom found to be a reason for high motivation. However, it must be remembered that the key factors of recognition, responsibility and rewarding work are usually the result of direct supervisor action. So while high morale people did not see the supervisor as a cause, the things that the supervisor had done were the important causes.

The supervisor must continue to recognize good work and reward this good work appropriately. In addition he will have to sharpen his skills in organizing and assigning the work so that the potential for achievement is always present and the work is interesting, challenging and meaningful.

What kind of a game would bowling be if there were a large curtain stretched across the alley a few feet beyond the balk line pulled only high enough to let the ball through?

How many good bowlers would you have? The easy answer is that there would be as many good ones, but what is considered "good" would be far inferior to standards of bowling as we know it. The standard of performance would surely be better if someone were positioned so that he could see behind the curtain and advise the competitor of the results he is producing and suggest changes and improvements.

Perhaps the bowling would not be much better, but this is where most supervisors stand in leadership today.

So leadership is changing in industry.

Where the leader once set goals for his people, defined the standards and the expected results, often today he participates with his people in goal setting and problem-solving.

Where he continually checked performance to make sure his people were doing things properly, he may now be expecting his people to check their own performance.

Where he disciplined his people to keep them in line, he now helps them see the need for rules and the ill effect of violations.

Where he was expected to develop and set in motion new methods of doing the job, today he may allow his people to help in job improvement.

Where he trained subordinates how to do the job, he now creates conditions in which learning can occur naturally.

Where he once pointed out failures and recognized achievement, he now helps people learn from their failures. He still recognizes achievement.

Chapter 10

The New Supervision
The Union-Free Work Group

The supervisor is the central figure in the union-free plant or office, even if his employer does not call on him to help actively in the counter-campaign, when a union is at the door. His greatest importance is in the long periods between campaigns. His actions, at best, will keep the organizer away; and at least will make the resistance easier if the organizers appear.

The "new" supervision is not the entire answer for the union-free workplace. The supervisor must be cautious in applying the new methods. The "motivator-dissatisfier" theory discussed earlier is a good example. This theory implies that all of the good things come from the motivators. The dissatisfier factors, it says, are of no great importance except when workers' expectations in the matter of fringe benefits, pay, working conditions and the like are not met.

This is a valuable concept to grasp. However, looking at the methods of union organizers, it is seen that an organizer feels at home with the dissatisfiers. This is his area of expertise. Dissatisfiers may lead disgruntled employees, unhappy with their work life, to seek out a union and ask its help in correcting the real or imagined wrongs.

So the supervisor in a union-free workplace must elevate the importance of the dissatisfiers. He must carefully eliminate factors that cause dissatisfaction, denying the organizer a handle on issues with which he can nurture discontent and unrest.

The organizer would be delighted to work in the area of the motivators, but he does not have the tools at his disposal. He has no way to grant employees achievement, recognition, responsibility, advancement, growth and fulfilling work (except those few to whom he can promise growth within the union's own organization). Besides, the motivators are not even easy to talk about, much less promise.

Responsibilities of the Supervisor

The supervisor's chief responsibility in preserving a union-free operation is maintaining a relationship with his people that will give him an accurate feeling of their attitudes and opinions and will give him advance warning of union activity. Closely allied to this is his responsibility for creating attitudes in his people that make them feel a union is unnecessary and, in fact, a little silly.

More specifically, the supervisor's responsibilities in a union-free plant may be classed in four ways: those regarding a) his people, b) the technical part of his job, c) the work environment, and finally, d) the company itself.

People

First, he must maintain everyday good supervision. He is not necessarily an emotional leader but should have a rapport such that his people will do an occasional unusual job as a favor to him. In many cases decisive votes against the union have been for no other purpose than to help out the supervisor. Over a period of time he will have shown that he has confidence in the integrity, ability and motivation of each one of the people under his supervision; he will have supported them, he will have coached and assisted them and he will at all times have been friendly and fair. He can expect mutual good feelings. At a minimum he will not be a "dissatisfying" factor.

Second, he must have built the relationship that is needed to gather accurate word about the feelings of the people he supervises and, through them, of workers throughout the plant or office. He must be informed on their expectations as to pay and benefits, compared with those the company is offering.

Above all, he must be tuned in to channels of information that will give him early warning of the presence among employees of union organizers: organizers visiting employees at home; handing out literature covertly; mailing union literature to homes; contacting employees at popular gathering places; etc. Rumors of any of these must be accorded respect.

Finally, he must establish himself as a credible person and a source of credible news and advice for his people.

All are of urgent importance. If a supervisor judges himself to be deficient in these and determines to bear down on one, it would be a difficult choice, but he should choose *early warning*. The company's counter-campaign is much more effective if begun in time. Note again that the advice we find everywhere on use of motivators is not emphasized here. High motivation in all the people is difficult to achieve and it waxes and wanes. It cannot be depended on to provide a defense against unionism.

Technical

The foreman's technical skill has only small relation to his ability to resist unionism. However, job knowledge is necessary to command respect and be the credible leader. The supervisor should have the knowledge needed to structure jobs that are interesting, challenging, even exciting.

Environment

The supervisor must supplement his communication contacts among the workers with a keen eye for sub-par working conditions, pay or fringe benefits. Again, he must have that rapport that will keep him informed on the expectations of his people.

The Company

The supervisor must have total understanding of his company's policy on unionism. He must have established channels of communication that will permit relay of good news, bad news and even news that may prove to be inconsequential.

He must know the company's policy on solicitation of employees and stand ready to enforce it strictly. If union handbills are being offered and are in compliance with solicitation rules, the supervisor should ask for one and get it to his boss.

Before any open solicitation occurs the supervisor should have learned of the union's activity. It is his responsibility to keep the management of the company informed. There are always signs of the union's presence before the open drive begins. Obviously there are signs such as a) discarded union material or authorization cards at work, b) an employee copying other employees' names from the clock cards, or c) a stranger conversing with employees outside the gate. It would pay the supervisor to know the faces of the organizers who are working his industry and area, if that is practical.

Added to these are an array of more subtle indicators based on shifting social ties and personal interaction. An otherwise amiable person may become sullen; small gatherings of employees, perhaps in unusual places, may be noted; workmanship may slip; a formerly popular worker may be "needled" by his mates; the "grapevine" may go dead; a former employee may appear outside regularly, right after work, buttonholing the workers going home; groups of employees may bring complaints to the supervisor, in a testy manner; new employees may proclaim, excessively, their loyalty to the company; an employee may defy, or show contempt for, his supervisor; groups may "clam up" when the supervisor approaches; an air of busyness may be noted in break times, where it had been relaxed; an employee may be getting a lot of attention from his fellow employees; a new "informal leader" may suddenly emerge; the supervisor may be asked probing questions about the company's personnel policies; and changing groupings and new cliques of employees may be observed.

The experienced supervisor may just feel it in his bones. But the warnings must not be ignored. He should get to the bottom of the out-of-pattern events and determine whether there is a union in the picture.

Training in Communication

Most of the things that the leader must do to meet his responsibility for keeping the workplace union-free have the common thread that he must communicate himself well. If he is to improve his own ability to meet his responsibility, he must improve his communicating. It is confusing in many ways to separate leadership and communication. Communication is so closely involved with leading—it may, in fact, be all of leading—that there is sure to be overlap when covering these two subjects. This chapter is concerned with personal communication technique. This is not a separate subject, but an addition to the study of leadership.

The first-line supervisor is only distantly involved with formal communication—the plant newspaper, the large group meeting, the employee newsletters and the letters to the homes of employees. He is much involved with communicating in his day-to-day actions. He interviews applicants and employees; he orients employees, reviews safety rules and practices, gives job instructions, makes work assignments, administers discipline, passes along company policies, interprets the more formal communications for his men and teaches. Teaching, a special type of communication, assumes high importance for the leader in a union-free operation.

The area of training most essential to staying union-free is the orientation that the supervisor gives new people in the department and new people in the company. The first few days on the job of an employee may well congeal his attitudes for the rest of his service. The effective supervisor has a planned reception that he will follow. The entire purpose of this plan is to show the new man, in effect, how to be an employee. First the supervisor must show him that he understands unusual or unexpected things may arise and must show an openness to questions about anything that puzzles him. The new man must be oriented physically. The location of the cafeteria, of the washroom, of the drinking fountains, his work routine are all simple things, but the new employee needs to know them to give him self-confidence, free of confusion and doubt.

He must give the new man a social reception. The newcomer has had no feel for the interrelations that exist among the people already at work. A man entering the labor market for the first time may not even know the proper relationship between himself and the boss. The people he is to work with may come from very different ethnic or national backgrounds from his own. In any event, they may have values that he does not understand. The supervisor must introduce him to each of the men and tell him enough about their backgrounds to enable him to start on a good social basis.

The supervisor must follow up strongly on the personal adjustment that the new man is making. If he doesn't seem to be making the social scene, the supervisor must help him.

Job instructions are basic. The union-free impact here is that the person who is "feeling his way" in a job without good instructions will have anxiety and a lack of confidence that can erode his morale. An assistant or another worker who has been checked out should be named the source of information for the new man in case the supervisor himself is not present. It is often wise to assign one of the old workers the duty of pairing with a new man to help him get a good start. This worker must be carefully selected and trained. Responsibility of this kind can be awarded to the regular worker as a symbol of achievement.

Many companies have a policy stating exactly what should be said to a new employee. In the absence of such a policy and where the foreman knows the company believes unionism is not in the best interest of its people, he should not hesitate to speak out about unionism to the new man. He should point out that the company offers work conditions that will make a union unnecessary, and give him reasons why a union may be undesirable: the union is not necessarily good for the employee, it makes the job less secure because the plant is less secure, it brings unpleasant relations and dissension and it makes strikes possible.

Upward Communication

The first inkling corporate management had that any trouble was afoot was an excited area supervisor reporting by long distance that he had received a telegram from a union business agent. It requested the company to bargain and claimed a majority of the employees had selected the union as their bargaining agent. The plant was one of several small petrochemical plants in the supervisor's area.

A familiar story came to light in the next few weeks as corporate labor relations staffers moved in to prepare for the election. The plant was under the supervision of a single salaried foreman. The foreman was of the old school. He was completely competent technically, followed orders without fail, operated the plant in a profitable manner and had good attitudes along with a deep loyalty to the company. He had joined the company as a common laborer many years before.

He would not hear of criticism of the company's policies or practices. He cursed subordinates, usually in a friendly way. He believed that everyone thought the same way about work as he did and that it made no difference how an order was given or what was being asked, it all paid the same.

He had known that there had been intermittent talk of getting a union in the plant, but he considered it just talk, intended to give him a scare. He had heard a rumor that a purse was being collected to send a man to visit the union at a sister plant of the company some two hundred miles distant. He had not heard whether anybody went. Three men had gone.

It later became clear that among the two or three leaders was the most competent workman in the plant, an "elder statesman". A man being groomed to become the next plant foreman.

The foreman had no intention of reporting matters to his boss that implied he did not have good command of his job. He had, in fact, made every effort to prevent any word of the approaching crisis from reaching higher levels by other channels.

His boss, the area supervisor, was not unmindful of his duty to stay in touch with all parts of his area of operations. He had heard via the grapevine and half-joking conversation with employees that all might not be well at the plant. He, too, had not the slightest intention of reporting to his corporate superiors that people under his wing were possibly being unionized. He contented himself with asking his foreman about it and received the stout denial he expected.

It had been very simple. A few of the men had invited a union in a nearby city (there was no local in the small town in which the plant was located) to represent them, promising a ready-made majority. A business agent then visited on several occasions, holding information meetings in employees' homes. In the process he convinced the leaders that they should work on making a "convert" of the key employee who was being trained for foreman, since all the people respected his opinion. This was accomplished. Authorization cards were secured from a majority of the employees and the business agent made his demand for recognition. The union won the election by a majority that was within one vote of the number he claimed at the outset in spite of massive last-minute efforts of corporate labor relations staffers to influence the outcome in favor of the company.

The great failure here was in the upward communication of the foreman and superintendent. They both knew the feeling of the workers involved, though perhaps only the superintendent suspected the *cause* of these feelings. Even more union-prone is the state of affairs in which the bad feelings are undetected and obvious causes are unobserved.

A 1967 survey of some 379 companies that had gone through union elections focused on the 281 losers. In a staggering 84 percent of them it was found that the management had had little or no idea of true employee opinion.

1. The management blamed the losses on wild union promises.

2. A study of the campaigns showed that the great single issue was wages.

3. These wage issues were in most cases based on non-factual comparison with other firms. They were often quite absurd and showed indifference on the part of the employee, as well as the union, to the economic needs of the company.

Now here it might be concluded that the cure for this situation would be to communicate the true facts to the people, who could then be expected to reject the union. But it is not that simple. The survey indicated that this demand for better wages was only a surface reason for joining the union. The real reason to most employees was the management's apparent coolness to employee complaints about their life at work. No real attempt had been made to deal with employee gripes. Most had, in fact, been totally ignored. *The employees were in a state of mind to accept the union's version of the facts and reject management's counter-arguments.* They appeared to be seizing on wages as something respectable to rally around and they were believing what they wanted to believe about wages, however farfetched.

4. Employee disenchantment with the company was found to have been actually caused by various unpalatable working conditions: poor food and eating spaces, dirty locker rooms, abusive supervisors (inconsiderate, unfair, harsh, bullying supervisors who did not permit them personal dignity), unreasonable shift schedules, unsanitary toilet facilities, cold and distant management, faulty vending machines and unanswered questions. It was *not* wages.

Some 25 percent of the losses were brought on by false or inaccurate information about management moves. The employees believed rumors and union charges that new machines, automation and reorganization were going to reduce jobs; that the plant or parts of the work were to be moved away; and that the work would be subcontracted. This sort of information had never been shared with employees, in most cases, by the management. The employees' beliefs were a surprise to the managers.

Management failures in resisting unionization, in this study, appeared to be due to employees' believing things that were not so. They believed incredible things because they harbored resentment of conditions at work. These conditions the management had made little effort to improve and had seemingly never heard about. The management and the supervision had not received sound upward communication. So it is a communication problem, but not the obvious kind. It is first of all an upward communication problem.

The Interview. Upward communication almost inevitably has to be one-on-one. All sorts of methods are available to the supervisor who would communicate to his men, group meetings, bulletin boards, individual notes, individual talks, but for upward communication the only practical method is the individual employee speaking to the individual foreman.

Thus, the techniques of interviewing are vital to good employee relations. Interviewing must not be thought of merely as screening new employees. There are techniques that can be mastered that will improve any formal discussion that the supervisor carries on with another person: the hiring decision interview, coaching (particularly the borderline performer), corrective or dismissal interview, performance review and salary interview (when pay is on a merit basis).

Before any interview the supervisor should set goals for himself. The goals should be in terms of the effects on the person who is being interviewed; the interviewee's behavior under a given set of conditions after the interview. This will save a great deal of blundering about.

Setting goals is part of the classic pattern of the formal interview. The pattern is usually five-step: preparation, establishing rapport, getting information, giving information and closing. In many types of interviews a sixth step, evaluation, may be added.

1. Setting goals is first in preparing for the interview. The next step is having a plan for conducting the interview and then, more specifically, thinking through a few specific questions or statements.

2. Establishing rapport, as the phrase is used in interviewing technique, is not the type of rapport that we think of between boss and worker in an ongoing relationship. In interviewing, getting rapport is simply putting the subject at ease in a setting in which he will be disposed to talk with freedom.

3. Getting information is not always among the goals of an interview, but where it is and where questions can be asked (in union organizing situations, when the union has started an open campaign, questioning of employees about union matters may bring on legal troubles), use the kind of questions that will yield the most information—questions that pose problems, seek opinion, ask clarification. Use questions that present alternatives or a list of ideas to choose from. Keep the conversation rolling by reflecting ideas, restating them in different words or interpreting them.

Interviewing advice is mostly concerned with what the interviewer says. But perhaps the best advice of all concerns that part of interviewing in which the interviewer says nothing. This is listening. Listen seriously. Listen for meaning. Try to read between the lines. Try to anticipate what your man is going to say. Above all, do not spend your listening time thinking of what you will say next.

Do not be afraid of silence. An experienced interviewer will learn that a long silence does not harm a one-on-one conversation. It places the burden squarely on the other person to speak and the thoughts conveyed at this point are sometimes the most valuable.

4. Giving information in an interview is no problem. But the interviewer must get feedback that assures him he is getting his message across.

5. The close. An interview in which information is sought, or information is being passed along, is simple to terminate. A simple "thank you" or a reason for leaving with the promise to get back together or a "let's think about it," will gracefully end most conversations. But the interview in which a meeting of the minds or some sort of agreement is sought is different. We must look to the salesman for help in this

situation. He might use a method such as *implied consent*: first getting agreement on broad generalizations which the worker appears to believe, then proceeding to the specific agreement that is wanted. Another step, if this does not go well, is to present alternatives, usually two ways of expressing the basic agreement which you seek. If there is clearly a strong objection to the result that is wanted, the *agreement but* gimmick can be brought into play. Here the supervisor agrees with the objection, or part of it, *but.* He then suggests another path to agreement.

Meetings and Writings

As far as the supervisor is concerned the best methods of communicating with groups are the meeting and the written document. The supervisor in the past was seldom called on to conduct small meetings of any great complexity. His meetings today are usually for instruction or simple passing of information. Times are changing. More and more, meetings with employees are being held in which new ideas and new approaches are solicited and today's supervisor should expose himself to this type of meeting. Leading this sort of meeting, where the outcome is unknown, is one of the new skills the supervisor needs to perform his job well. The important part of a meeting is, as in the interview, the setting of goals to be reached, prior to the meeting itself.

Meetings may result in molding a closeknit group, regardless of subject matter or the skill of the meeting leader. In studies of effective work groups, the holding of meetings of any kind appeared to promote the group's effectiveness.

The use of written communications is largely a matter of common sense. Items of relative permanence or items of complexity are ordinarily transmitted in writing. Examples of this are the department's rules, operating instructions for a complex machine, safety signs, a new procedure or an old one. Why should workers be given lengthy training to learn a checklist, when the checklist itself can be posted at the job site? To resist a union campaign, a company may use many forms of written communications. The foreman, though, will not often be called on to communicate with his people in writing about the union's organizing attempts, but will use oral, man-to-man techniques.

Rapport, Feedback

An organizing drive was going well at a television station and a union victory seemed assured. The union already had a foothold in a radio station operated by the owners of the television facility.

A supervisor discovered in a casual conversation that the union had promised a few of the longer-service television employees a unified seniority list with the radio station. He reported his finding to management, pointing out that the television group was a much younger crowd, on the whole, than the radio group.

A quick-hitting bulletin board message exposed the plan. The union added to its troubles by switching positions, confirming the company and losing the support of those who would have been helped by a unified list. The election was a formality, NO UNION winning handily.

Here feedback on the issues of a union campaign, passed up the line by an alert foreman, meant the difference between defeat and victory for the company. On other occasions feedback from supervisors on people in the voting group has been vital. For example, learning of the disaffection of a key man might trigger special efforts to win him over.

Feedback from the workers on union plans, union progress, and issues are obviously of high value to the company. Finally, feedback on employee opinion, attitudes, their objections to the union, their complaints and dissatisfaction about working conditions and disliked supervisors and managers are indispensable in waging an effective counter-campaign. The give and take of personal conversation will ultimately determine the amount and value of the feedback that the foreman gets.

The supervisor will often find himself on the receiving end of pressures and dissatisfactions of the workers caused by such factors as the company's policies, procedures, rules, regulations, promotions, growth opportunities and physical conditions. The pressure must be borne by the foreman, even though these are exactly the things over which he has least control. By the same token, the managers who are most responsible for making changes in these factors are least able to know about the problem. The supervisor must be prepared to communicate about these problems. Here again it is foremen communication, this time upward *and* downward that is the answer.

In his person-to-person leadership of his group, the supervisor should aim at creating or maintaining a living community built on trust and at using the full resources and abilities of the workers. He should work on "leveling" as a means of getting his people to make known their abilities, as well as their needs. He should demonstrate that he can be trusted and that any information they offer will be used to help them.

Feedback is a two-way street. Besides feeding back to the worker the obvious information about the job and the company, the supervisor often would like to give facts designed to change workers' behavior. He knows that at times he must "unfreeze" behavior that is undesirable and install new behavior that is more useful. When the feedback must be criticism, it should emphasize here-and-now occurrences. It should not evaluate the person, judge or interpret. Some specifics about rapport-feedback are:

1. Questions and requests should always be answered. Even if the answer is no or the request denied, the supervisor should show that he has done something. Even if he is too busy at the moment to answer he should inform his employee of this, not brush him off. Employees should be consulted for their opinions and ideas. The action taken on an idea or suggestion should be fed back even if it is negative.

2. The supervisor should be approachable and show that he cares and wants to help. He must listen and show that he is listening and he understands what is being said. If he can't help he should tell why.

The Grapevine

Every organization will have a grapevine. People want to know more about what is going on and they will find unofficial sources, even where official channels are giving adequate information. To use the grapevine, the supervisor must have a picture of its organization. He must identify the "news carriers" in the grapevine and deliberately tune himself in. The grapevine, at least that network in which he is interested, is for non-management communication. He may learn things about working conditions that will surprise him—and enable the company to head off a possible source of dissatisfaction.

Another dimension is added when the supervisor learns to use the grapevine for his own communication. This is a delicate process and it must be only sparingly used. Certainly specific instructions should never be passed in this way. However, if there is a problem that would be hard to handle with a general announcement or notice, such as absenteeism, the grapevine might help. A word to the effect that a crackdown is in the wind, dropped so that it can be picked up by the news carrier, may be all that is needed.

Concern-Orientation

"Bill, you are our boss. Tell me, is there any chance for me to ever get a supervisor's job without a college degree? I don't mean to gripe, but I've been operating this position for three years now and I don't see any way to get ahead."

"I've had it up to here! Nobody in the so-called management gives a damn what happens to a man. I've tried for three years to find some way to get ahead. I give up; there's no way to get a fair deal. You can tell them what they can do with this job!"

These two quotations demonstrate the difference between a concern and a complaint. The difference is about a month, if the concern is not acted on. Most complaints that the supervisor hears have been forerun by a concern that he has also heard, but has done little about.

The supervisor who doesn't listen and doesn't act undercuts his own authority. The employee may go on to higher command or seek help outside the company, but even if he simply drops the subject, he will likely not go to the supervisor again.

The supervisor should strive always to act on the concerns he hears or senses. Even when he knows the solution is beyond his power, he must get the concern or complaint straight and make sure exactly what the problem is. He should show his own concern for the problem if it is a legitimate concern, but he should show his concern for the state of mind of his employee even if he feels there is no real basis for the problem.

The supervisor who allows himself to be oriented only to complaints will multiply those complaints. The concern-oriented supervisor leads the more serene life at work.

A Check-Up

Every supervisor should periodically take a long look at his own performance as a communicator. Most times he will find he is not doing the job he is capable of. He should answer for himself such questions as:

Are my employees getting information about the use of company products? The way wages are determined? The background and philosophy of the company? Important new orders or business? Plans to build? New products? New research and development in the company? Who the important customers are? How sales are going? How our department is doing its part?

Are employees told of production plans and schedules that have been set up? Employment plans for the months ahead? Organization changes, before they are released to the public press? The standing of the company in its industry?

Do I discuss such subjects with employees as operating problems? Customer complaints? The company's financial situation? The costs of doing business? The need for advertising? The role of shareowners? The "break-even" point? Customer complaints? The importance of productivity? The role of competition?

Do employees understand the problems of financing the business? The function of company executives? The importance of profits? The importance of their individual jobs? The real meaning of job security?

Are the benefits and advantages of working for the company discussed with employees? Do they know of efforts to stabilize employment in bad times? Are the broad issues of our economic system discussed with employees—government spending? The burden of taxes? The fact that machines make jobs? The causes of inflation? The need for both big and small businesses? The achievements of the American enterprise system?

Do employees get a real opportunity to ask questions and get honest answers? Do they get explanations in terms of facts, rather than opinion or conclusions? Do employees see their job responsibilities in writing? Do employees know all about advancement opportunities? Does the employee know how he stands, what his strong points are and what points he needs improvement in? Is there a regular method for learning employees' views, opinions and attitudes? Do I actually have regular informal talks with employees?

Most important, do employees know the company's view on unionism? Solicitation rules? The whys of union-free operation?

Conclusion

We see that most of the responsibilities of the supervisor in maintaining union-free conditions seem to shake down to *communicating*. The company needs early warning of union activity. It needs to know the concerns of the workers. It needs employees who know the company's feeling on union activity and who are inclined to oppose the union's move for power. It needs motivated individuals and effective groups.

The company cannot have these things unless supervisors communicate ably.

Chapter 11

The New Supervision
Ideas that Work

Having looked at the new skills required of today's supervisors and the special abilities needed in the union-free workplace, we can move to specific ideas used by successful supervisors. These turn out to be ways to improve, one way or another, personal relations with workers, to create the rapport that is so vital to their feeling no need for union representation.

This is only a sampling of many ideas that are being used, ideas that can work to smooth the path for the supervisor. One work situation is never just like any other; the supervisor will know quickly that certain of the ideas will have no application to this job. Perhaps none of them can be carried over unchanged to his job, but one or two may trigger related ideas for the alert supervisor. The important thing is to be open to new ideas and suggestions and be willing to try them out.

The effective supervisor will look at them closely to find a "fit" that he can put to work in his own situation. He will always be weighing the ideas of others. He will not hesitate to try new ideas, always within the scope of his authority, of course.

Written Aids

People Book

Many successful supervisors keep a pocket notebook for recording personal facts about their workers, not a mass of intimate detail but the off-the-job information that sets each of them apart as an individual. His family situation, his hobbies, his outside civic work, his birthday, anniversary, places he has worked and lived, his hometown, his neighborhood, his wife's name, the names and ages of his children, their interests and accomplishments, all should be recorded. Does he own his home? Live in an apartment? Own his own car? What is his religion? Does he have serious financial troubles? What are his concerns about the job?

Having the facts straight is a great aid to conversation and in showing one's concern and interest in the individual. Many bosses shy away from personal inquiry for fear of asking the wrong questions or showing ignorance or confusion in a matter such as the ages or sex of the man's children. Gathering these facts is not for the purpose of manipulating people, but to provide them the kind of leadership they need and want.

Work Record

A more formal document than the "people book", a work record showing job-related data is kept by many a supervisor for each of his people. This record frankly duplicates much that can be found in company records, but it includes in one place most of the facts that the supervisor may need from time to time. The data should be entered on a standard form, so facts can be located quickly. They might include such items as:

1. Personal Data—name, address, telephone number, birthday, date of hire, accrued seniority.
2. Employment Record—changes in jobs, wage history, shift, transfers.
3. Absence and Health Record—all absences, including sickness and notation of important health problems.
4. Discipline Record—all disciplinary action and warning, together with the nature of the offense and the date.
5. Grievances—a brief notation of the grievances filed by the employee and their settlement.
6. Merit and Award Record—all special commendations for merit or achievement, awards for suggestions, length of service and safety performance.
7. Performance Record—each employee is appraised regularly and a summary of the findings is entered in the work record. If the job has a production standard, the percentage record is entered. Events—goals, training plans, etc.—that would bear on the next formal appraisal are noted.

8. Ability Record—special skills are noted. A summary of early work experience and training that may help in making an assignment, or promotion, is included.

Daily Plan

A plan in writing of each day's work (or longer period, depending on the work cycle) can dramatically improve a supervisor's efficiency. It can also improve his rapport with his people. The plan should earmark time for each day's tasks, systematically covering the job's goals (sorting out the *important few* actions from the *trivial many*) and accounting for four types of events: a) Daily Routine—the routine chores, channeling each action toward the priority matters. Note deadlines for reports. Set aside visiting time with workers at work stations. b) Predictable Unknown—perhaps the boss will ask for a special report; perhaps an unusual order will have to be handled; things that are bound to occur, but what and when are unknown. c) Periodical Known—an equipment failure, an interview of an applicant where what, but not when, is known. A category of necessary, but deferrable, actions in each day's plan will provide the needed cushion to take care of these and predictable unknowns as they arise. d) Emergency—giving advance attention to more predictable events makes emergencies less a problem for the time budget.

The experienced supervisor will attempt, where practical, to defer to the next day's plan the problem discovered today. This not only allows time to execute today's plan, but often makes the solution easier with additional time, information and thought. The daily plan will provide for work on employees' problems and questions and for paperwork on employee records, insurance claims, etc.

Calendar

A write-in calendar or card bring-up system will enhance any supervisor's results. Besides an unfailing ability to "remember" deadlines and meetings that the work requires, the calendar provides a follow-up on personal contacts with workers, claims and inquiries that are going through channels on behalf of employees, birthdays and anniversaries.

Informal Notes

Some successful supervisors have used short notes as a means of staying in touch with their people to supplement face-to-face contact.

At times when praise or a compliment is to be passed along, the written note is used for its lasting effect. Knowing that a copy of the note will be in his permanent file is a source of pride to an employee.

Another use of informal notes is writing postcards or letters to the employee's home about work-connected matters such as a change in schedule, a rule that affects the employee, or a change in policy that would be of particular interest to him.

A note may be no more than a request to "ask me about this next time we get together," but it cements relationships and builds bridges.

Technology

Not strictly "written" aids, but serving similar purposes, are two tools of great potential not yet in general use by supervisors: the cassette recorder and the polaroid camera.

The Cassette Recorder

Small enough to carry strapped to the belt, the cassette recorder can serve as secretary on the supervisor's regular rounds; it can be used to record operating instructions for a new piece of equipment as the factory states them and on *all* equipment for the new man coming into the section (here the supervisor conducts a guided "tour" of the equipment and each new man gets the same full information); to record witnesses' statements about an accident or incident and on and on. The cost of one of these is such that the supervisor need not wait for his employer to purchase one, he can swing it himself.

The Instant Camera

This instrument is particularly useful for pinpointing cluttered work areas, safety threats, unsafe practices and, on the lighter side, for picturing the workers at work and at recreation to enliven bulletin boards.

The Personal Bulletin Board

This is an idea which has caught on recently, though some supervisors have used it for years. This is not the company's bulletin board, but a board at the supervisor's desk on which he posts reminders, slogans, his own schedule, the organization chart and on which workers can leave notes for him, requests to see him, messages left for him, information he needs, etc.

Employees' Bulletin Board

Another bulletin board idea is the board for the personal use of the employees. This board would carry want-ad-type messages, humorous material, requests to swap shifts, clippings about members of the group, photos from vacation trips, general invitations, thank-you notes for gifts or cards the group has sent and matters of this sort. It is for the use of employees and the supervisor would not post anything on it, except through one of the employees.

Task Forces

A new way for the supervisor to build work group team spirit is the forming of committees and task forces to cope with problems connected with the work and to handle off-the-job activities. Posts of leadership of the small groups can be awarded for good performance. A safety committee, a work study committee, a housekeeping committee, even a grievance committee are possible on-the-job groups. They would meet and function under the general lead of the supervisor. Off the job, there might be a social committee, a sports committee, a memorials committee and a visit-the-sick group. The committees should cut across the regular work groups and they should *not* be elected, since there is no intent that they should represent employees, only accomplish tasks, surveys, studies or inspections and make recommendations. Legal problems can arise if such a group functions as a representative. This might be considered a "company union" by the NLRB.

Oral Communication

Ombudsman

The European idea of the ombudsman in government may have its uses in the workplace. This is a person who acts as a go-between, solving citizen's problems that relate to the government, helping people to get the service from the government to which they are entitled. The best arrangement would have the supervisor as the ombudsman for his work group, working between the group and the company. Some supervisors have been able to establish just this relationship. But employees are often unwilling to bring tough questions and complaints to the boss. A more workable form, one that has been installed company-wide by at least one national company, is the appointment of a worker from the ranks to act as go-between. This would be a person who has the confidence of his fellow workers. He would serve a term of six months or more then rotate out, to give another the experience. On assuming the go-between role, the employee is thoroughly checked out in company personnel policies and benefits. He works on such widely differing problems as settling disputes between workers, getting estimates of pension benefits and payout options and handling complaints. He will handle most cases through the supervisor, not direct with the staff people who have the information. Where the supervisor has installed this system on his own hook, *all* matters would be handled with him by the ombudsman; he will then make the necessary contacts with staff people and will adjust complaints to the best of his ability, always channeling the results back through the ombudsman. The supervisor would forego none of his usual contacts with his people in this system. Hopefully, he will learn of problems through the ombudsman that would not have surfaced in the usual way.

Rap Sessions

Companies have found executive rap sessions valuable in times when there is an apparent morale problem and a possible union threat. This is a program in which higher executives meet small groups of employees with no immediate supervision present, in what is, frankly, a gripe session. The men are assured that they may speak freely without reprisal. Sometimes an outside consultant may be brought in to conduct these sessions. Either way, any ideas for improving conditions at the workplace are reviewed at once by management and action is taken.

There is no reason to wait for trouble to use this upward communication tool, nor to wait for a company program. The supervisor can invite higher managers in the plant to meet with his people to field questions, explain company programs and financial problems and answer gripes and complaints. Again, only the single executive should meet with the workers. No openness can be expected with others, particularly the supervisor, present.

Listening

The problem with listening is that a person can think and understand about four times as fast as anyone can talk. Typically, the extra time goes to mind-wandering or thinking of a reply. The experts suggest trying to guess the next thought or idea. No harm is done if the guess is wrong. Then weigh the evidence or reasoning being offered. Occasionally recap in the mind all that has been said. Finally, if the talk is one-to-one, feed back the thought in different words.

Patterned Conversation

If the problem is rapport and it is hard to imagine how rapport can be *too* good, systematically buttonholing employees in pre-planned patterned conversation can open the channels. In this system the supervisor allots time in each day's plan for work-connected conversations with the workers. The subjects may be varied. The conversation is best kicked off with open questions of the type used in interviewing. Questions might be in three categories: seeking information, asking for suggestions and soliciting opinion.

Information
"What do you remember about _____?" "Can you explain what happened in _____?" "Tell me how it looked to you." "How did it happen that _____?"

Suggestions
"How do you think we should handle this?" "You know what this equipment is supposed to do; how do you think we should operate it?" "I have a problem—the facts are these _____. What would you do if you were in my shoes?" "I have been thinking about this new idea: _____. How do you evaluate it?"

Opinion
"Why did this happen, in your opinion?" "What do they mean by _____?" "Would you say that _____?" "Now that you have had a chance to work on _____, what do you think of it?" "_____ looks like _____ that happened a couple of months ago. How do you compare them?"

This kind of questioning is designed, first, to open up a work-connected conversation. Problems can be solved. New problems can be uncovered early. But they also provide the worker with recognition and the grand feeling that his ideas count for something.

Fruitful Questioning

The supervisor can construct his own questions by mastering the patterns used by skilled interviewers. An important part of successful questioning is in the way things are said, the phrasing. Avoid words that anger, by using neutral words—*disagreed,* not *fought; disliked,* not *hated; lacked skill,* not *incompetent.* Use softening entry words—"To what do you attribute _____?" "Would you say that _____?" "Is it possible that _____?" Avoid questions that produce little information—"In what ways is this _____?" rather than "Is this _____?" Reassure—"That happens often."

Things will move when the supervisor frames his approach wisely:

Open-End Question

"What is your experience with _____?" "How do you think we should handle this?" "Do you have any ideas on _____?" This kind of question gives the man a chance to compose a complete answer. It pays respect to his ability and it usually will earn his cooperation.

The Negative Question

A disaster in sales, the negative question is often a winner in worker relations. It allows a man to get off the hook if he wants to: "Joe, I don't suppose you'd want to put in two or three extra hours tonight in the tool crib?" If Joe wants to work he can do so, feeling that he is performing above and beyond the call of duty. If not, it has been made easy for him to refuse.

Problem Question

"What would you do if _____?" "Suppose _____, how would you handle it?" A question setting up an imaginary situation is a great opener. Your man talks easily and is apt to contribute creatively.

Tail-End Question

This is a form in which a tough statement or order is given, but with a question mark at the end: "I know those tolerances are tight, but we have to get that order out this afternoon. Okay?" This takes the sting out of an order and makes the conversation two-way, if the worker wants it to be.

Indirect Questioning

"What would you say are the biggest problems workers have in getting along together?" A question put like this may reveal to you how easily he gets along.

Question-and-Planted-Answer

"How about trying it this way?" This give the individual the chance to voice his opinions, but along lines that you have indicated would be productive. At the same time the supervisor signals his openness to criticism or contradiction, if it is necessary.

The Summary Question

The supervisor will find it rewarding in many cases to review for the worker what has taken place. To the lab technician the group leader says "Joe, is it understood after you have completed the routine on this batch you will check back with me with the report of your findings?" If Joe has any questions or doubts he can then bring them up.

Come Off Courteous

A supervisor kids himself if he thinks his people do not expect courtesy. Others may believe they are courteous when in fact their words and tone do not add up to courtesy.

Giving Orders

The best supervisors give orders as a request. It is a special kind of bland request which both he and the worker know is an order. He thanks him for doing as he had "asked." "Please" and "thank you" have been called the magic words of leadership.

Appealing to Pride

"Joe, you have had a fine record with the company all along. How would you like to add another achievement to the list? If you can work out a way to speed up this . . . we would use your technique for a long time . . ."

Recognizing his Contribution

"Thank you, John, for the fine job you did in training that young Smith boy. It will be some time before he gets up to your class, but you have given him a good start."

Personal Touch

Two techniques will help the supervisor maintain a close personal touch with his people: contacts outside work and work appraisal.

Togetherness

Military leadership theory holds that the leader should in most ways hold himself aloof from his people, as much as possible avoid contacts outside the command situation. This is not believed the best practice in industry. If there is any application of it, it is that the leader in industry should not become, or appear to become, especially close with one or two of his people. When this happens, there is no way to be even-handed enough to keep the others from believing he is favoring his friends.

The effective supervisor will deliberately cultivate contacts with his people outside work, in social situations and in community group activity. He will discuss work problems by telephone after hours with his men, but not the critical things, nor matters that would lead to a lengthy discussion. He will call with information about starting times or items that should be brought to work. He will, on occasions, drop notes of congratulation or best wishes if appropriate; comment on something he has seen in the newspaper about the man or his family, perhaps enclosing the clipping, since an extra one may be wanted by the family.

Performance Review

Most companies do not have performance appraisal programs that reach all the way to the work bench, operating position or office desk. Though usually reserved for managers, supervisors and professionals, work appraisal and appraisal-sharing have their uses at the other end of the ladder, too.

A fair, objective work review can be expected to produce certain good results with an employee. He will know where he stands; he will understand his job better; he will know how his work is regarded; and he will have a challenge for the future.

But there is danger in reviewing performance with employees. Most of the plans that get into trouble are those judging traits or assessing an employee's worth, overall. These measurements, whether they be rank orders, mathematical coding, letter grades or check marks on a graduated scale, will lead to difficulties. The successful systems judge the work, not the worker. They are keyed on performance. They are based on the employee's success in reaching results, which results are measurable and have been agreed upon as the measure of his success. A written record of the performance review is kept.

Other objections are being raised to employee appraisals. No one doubts the morale value and motivating power of a favorable appraisal. But some authorities believe that no unfavorable appraisal should be passed on to an employee. Even when it is disguised as a failure to reach agreed on goals, the employee will know the company's view of him is unfavorable. The performance review, according to this view, should be favorable in those areas where performance has been good enough, but should only counsel for improvement in the other areas.

Job Action

The supervisor has means at his disposal to enrich the working life of his people and to make them more effective persons.

Job Enrichment

Where the jobs are repetitive and simple the supervisor finds it a challenge to make the work interesting, let alone exciting. There are things he can try. He can train his men to anticipate emergencies, to become proficient in all jobs in the department and to be able to advance to supervision if vacancies occur. He can make them responsible for quality checks and tests; he can find programmed instruction courses in the basics of the engineering or science that is involved in the job.

Job Posting

In companies that do not routinely post vacant jobs for bid, the supervisor can do it on his own. Postings enable employees to know that they are considered for every job for which they feel themselves qualified. Highly motivated employees who might somehow be overlooked are considered and un-interested people are not presented with an agonizing decision by being offered a promotion they would not have sought out. Job posting can also be used for filling favorable shifts as they become vacant or for other moves that are not in the nature of promotion.

Overtime Rotation

If his company has no system for rotating overtime the supervisor can set up a list that will guarantee that overtime is spread fairly. Where overtime is sought eagerly, the eligible worker with the least hours of overtime is offered the hours. If he does *not* accept he is credited with the number of hours worked by the man who does accept. If overtime is generally avoided, the system is run in reverse. The man with the least is expected to work the hours unless he has good reason not to and no hours are credited to him if he fails to work.

Contests

The supervisor can arouse group excellence by having competitions within his own area and offering prizes to the winners. The prize

might be a product "promoted" from the company, a small gift cer-
tificate, nothing too expensive, since the recognition is the important
factor here. The subject of the contest in the group might be a
company-wide emphasis, such as soliciting credit card applications in
an oil company; housekeeping, using a point system over a period of
time, to maintain interest; or work improvement suggestions. The
possibilities are endless.

It may be advisable to recognize daily and weekly winners, each
award consisting of a chance in a drawing for a grand prize. The drawing would be held at longer intervals, perhaps at a social gathering,
and everyone by that time should have at least one chance at the big
prize. This maintains the interest of all.

Work Simplification

The system called Work Simplification, designed for the prime purpose of raising efficiency, has been found to produce high morale and
high interest in jobs. The workers do the simplification, usually in
groups on company time. There are five basic steps in this kind of
work improvement: a) zero in on single job or task to be improved; b)
get the facts, and if the flow of work is complex, make a chart of it;
and c) challenge every detail. Of each operation, ask what is its purpose? Why is it necessary? Where should it be done? When should it be
done? Who should do it? How should it be done for best results?

Recruiting

To predict the work attitudes of a high school graduate, talk to his
teachers. Studies by a major corporation disclosed high correlation
between teachers' and company's judgments of habits, cooperation,
performance and absenteeism. The study concluded that "Whatever it
is that determines a supervisor's evaluation of work performance, the
high school teacher measures it more successfully than standard ap-
titude tests."

Grievance Handling

The supervisor in a union-free plant must keep his handling of
grievances above reproach. The supervisor who takes care of complaints, concerns and gripes with gravity has a lot going for him. His
people will then be more inclined to voice their concerns and the
supervisor will be able to keep discontent at low levels. This is the best
a grievance handling system can do. The supervisor is dealing in the

dissatisfiers when he handles grievances and we have seen the great danger that the dissatisfiers may trigger a union movement among the workers.

Restating

One of the few gimmicks in industrial relations that really works is the advice to the supervisor to get a grieving worker to restate his grievance, several times if necessary, for full clarity. Then the supervisor states the problem back to him in his own words. Many grievances will die right there. Perhaps the worker has only wanted a hearing; perhaps the grievance has fallen of its own weight; or perhaps the answer has emerged, but in any case the grievance is often settled and in the best way.

Work Group Grievance Plan

In those companies that do not have a formal grievance process the supervisor can set up his own. This will not be a formal plan but just a clear understanding that the worker should voice his complaints, with the promise that submitting grievances will not be considered some kind of disloyalty or bad attitude. The key to success in a grievance plan is a two-way feeling of trust. In a union-free operation the grievance procedure that has no grievances is a failure.

The supervisor should arrange with a respected member of his own higher management to act as a judge of a worker's appeal of his decision. The judge acts as the analog of the arbitrator in a union grievance procedure.

Grievance Log

The grievance log book, often successful in a plant-wide setting, can be applied to a supervisor's work group. In use, this is a record kept by the foreman of any grievances or requests for information that he cannot handle on the spot. There will be space for writing the final disposition of the case. Where there is a plant-wide program the log books of the various supervisors will be reviewed daily by higher supervision to assure that problems are being handled properly. The advantage of such a system, even when one leader is operating it and there is no review, is that the employee does not have to do any writing, as in the usual formal grievance system. This is sometimes a major hurdle for the employee to get over. In this, and in all systems recommended, the employee is allowed, even encouraged, to bring another employee to help him with his grievance or inquiry.

An urgent emphasis is placed on bringing grievances into the open. Failing to provide an outlet for employees' questions about their work life is a near-fatal flaw in a program of labor relations. A failure here frustrates the workers and makes them easy targets for a union organizer. Indeed, it alone might cause them to *seek out* a union. A well-run grievance handling system, on the other hand, pulls the teeth of this favorite promise of the organizers.

Conclusion

The supervisor in the union-free plant, office or shop has the special responsibility of seeing that his own work group does not become the center of discontent that paves the way for a union. He must also create those conditions, as we have seen, that will enable him to have early warning of organizing attempts and to have a feel for the overall morale and temper of the employees in all work groups.

This doesn't just happen. It is the result of the leader's knowing what skills he needs, what his responsibilities are and, finally, translating what he knows into action. To help him get action is the purpose of listing these specific ideas that the supervisor might install.

It may be asked if these techniques do not amount to manipulation of workers. Not so. There is no exploiting of people, no deception, only actions directed toward giving them a better life at work. This, plus better employee knowledge about unionism, should achieve the company's goal of a union-free operation.

Again, it may be that none of these ideas can be put in without modification. But whether these or completely different ideas are carried out, the supervisor's final responsibility is to *act*. He must not wait for trouble to break out. The time is now.

Chapter 12

Labor Law
& the Union-Free Supervisor

This is a guide to the types of activity that a supervisor should be able to recognize as danger areas in the defense against a union's efforts to organize his people. It should not be considered legal advice; such advice should be obtained in the usual manner.

James L. Dougherty

Don't promise employees a pay increase, promotion, benefit or special favor if they stay out of the union. Don't threaten loss of jobs, reduction of income, etc. or use intimidating language. Don't threaten or actually discharge, discipline or layoff. Don't threaten to close or move the plant or reduce operations. Don't threaten, through a third party, any of the above. Don't spy on union meetings. Don't conduct yourself in a way which would indicate you are watching employees to determine whether they are participating in union activities. Don't discriminate against employees actively supporting the union by assigning undesirable work.

Listening intently, the newly appointed supervisor mentally agrees he will not do any of these unsavory acts as they are spotlighted, one by one, by the speaker (a training specialist from company headquarters). He is gathered with other supervisors to learn about union organizing drives, which may soon threaten the union-free status of his plant.

Don't transfer employees prejudicially because of union affiliation. Don't engage in partiality favoring non-union employees. Don't discipline or penalize employees actively supporting a union for an infraction which non-union employees are allowed to commit. Don't make any work assignment for the purpose of causing an employee to quit his job. Don't take any action that is intended to impair the status of, or adversely affect an employee's job or pay. Don't assign work or transfer men so that those active in behalf of a union are separated from those you believe do not favor the union. Don't select employees to be laid off with the intention of curbing the union's strength.

The new supervisor stirs uneasily in his auditorium chair. He is trying to think of some normal act in his range of duties that would not be impaired, if a union were at the gates.

Don't ask employees for an expression of their thoughts about a union. Don't ask employees how they intend to vote. Don't ask employees at time of hiring or thereafter whether they belong to a union. Don't ask employees about the internal affairs of unions such as meetings, plans, etc. Don't make a statement that you will not deal with the union. Don't make statements to employees to the effect that they will be discharged or disciplined for unionism. Don't urge employees to try to persuade others to oppose the union. Don't prevent employees from soliciting union memberships during their free time on company premises. Don't give financial support or assistance to any union. Don't visit the homes of employees for the purpose of urging them to reject the union. Don't make speeches to assemblies of employees on company time within the 24-hour period before opening of the polls. Don't speak to an employee about the union campaign or urge him to vote against the union, in your office or the office of another management official. Don't help employees to withdraw union memberships. Don't ask employees about the identity of the instigator or leader of employees favoring the union.

What would an alert young supervisor who has been exposed to all these tabus do, when his group of workmen are wooed by a union organizer? Chances are good he would resolve that he must keep his mouth shut, must keep clear of the whole dangerous business of talking, even casually, about the union. Worse yet, he reads from the handouts he receives at the training session:

Sec. 8(a) It shall be an unfair labor practices for an employer

(1) to interfere with, restrain, or coerce employees in the exercise of the rights guaranteed in Section (7);

(2) to dominate or interfere with the formation or administration of any labor organization or contribute financial or other support to it. . .

(3) by discrimination in regard to hire or tenure of employment or any term or condition of employment to encourage or discourage membership in any labor organization. . .

(4) to discharge or otherwise discriminate against an employee because he has filed charges or given testimony under this Act;

(5) to refuse to bargain collectively with the representatives of his employees. . .

The supervisor will be deep in his shell by now. When one of his people asks him for his opinion about having a union, he will smile mysteriously and say, "no comment."

No supervisor wants to violate a law of the federal government and his company won't ask him to. In labor law the difficulty is knowing what the law is. The law speaks in generalities, and its interpretation by the National Labor Relations Board and the courts, in thousands of rulings, has left us with a long list of "no-no's". We can't even be confident that a particular action, legal today, will continue so, since these interpretations can be changed as casually as they were established.

So the supervisor who wants to inform himself on the best way to act during a union organizing drive will come on these "don'ts" and these lists of unfair labor practices everywhere he turns. Companies within the jurisdiction of the NLRB, in putting together a crash course for supervisors when the union organizer knocks, will almost invariably place the emphasis on the countless actions the supervisor must *not* perform, so the company will not be embroiled in legal trouble.

This may be self-defeating behavior by a company. The foreman must not be neutralized in an organizational drive. He is the key to successful resistance. Freeing him to reach his full potential for influencing and guiding his people to vote "NO UNION" is no great risk for a company. The laws actually place minimal restrictions on his normal activity; most of the unfair labor practices are not his to commit, as we shall see.

The Supervisor Defined

But first, what is a supervisor and what does being a supervisor mean, in the eyes of the Labor Management Relations Act? The House Report on H. R. 3020, the bill that led to the Taft-Hartley Act said,

Supervisors are management people. They have distinguished themselves in their work. They have demonstrated their ability to take care of themselves without depending upon the pressure of collective action. No one forced them to become supervisors. They abandoned the "collective security" of the rank and file voluntarily, because they believed the opportunities thus opened to them to be more valuable to them than such "security." It seems wrong, and it is wrong, to subject people of this kind, who have demonstrated their initiative, their ambition and their ability to get ahead, to the leveling processes of seniority, uniformity and standardization that the Supreme Court recognizes as being fundamental principles of unionism. . . It is wrong for the foremen, for it discourages the things in them that made them foremen in the first place. For the same reason, that it discourages those best qualified to get ahead, it is wrong for industry, and particularly for the future strength and productivity of our country.

On the job, a supervisor might be defined as one who has authority to direct employees or to discipline them, assign them, adjust their grievances, hire, fire, transfer, suspend, lay off, recall, promote or reward them. These are also the definitions used in the Act and anyone having any one of these responsibilities or the power effectively to recommend such action is a supervisor. However, his supervisory duty must involve the exercise of independent judgment and not be merely routine or under close supervision of others. Time study men, "straw bosses", leadmen and set-up men are usually not considered supervisors.

In borderline cases other factors are considered, such as a) job title, b) the fact he is thought of by others as a supervisor, c) his privileges, d) attendance at meetings and training sessions of supervisors, e) responsibility for a shift or a particular operation, f) reception of orders direct from management, not through other supervisors, g) responsibility for communicating management's instructions to employees, h) inspection responsibility, i) training responsibility, j) authority to give leaves of absence, k) responsibility for reporting violations of rules, l) freedom from punching the time clock, m) freedom from regular production or maintenance duties and n) wearing different work clothes from the regular employees.

Education has no bearing on supervisory status, and exemption from Fair Labor Standards regulation is only a secondary factor, as shown by rulings of the NLRB that engineers laying out the work of crews but not supervising them, engineers who did studies but had authority only to recommend action and engineers who could call on lower-ranked engineers for assistance but had only technical guidance authority were not supervisors within the meaning of the Act.

This, then, is the supervisor: the employer can discipline him for his own union activity (he is not protected by the law in self-organizing, unless the discipline intimidates or threatens regular, non-supervisory employees) and the employer may require him to actively oppose the activities of union organizers. The employer may be held responsible for a supervisor's statements or actions which add up to an unfair labor practice or interference with the Board's election process. This is why employers so often overburden their supervisors with "don'ts".

But how wise is teaching the "don'ts"? Only three of the five unfair labor practices are of any importance to the union-free plant or shop and of these only one is important to the first-line supervisor. Even if he oversteps the bounds on this one, the penalty will almost certainly not be an order to bargain with the union, only the posting of a notice and a rerun of the election.

The Unfair Labor Practices

The unfair labor practices of "domination of a union" and "discrimination" against an employee for filing charges are seldom charged against the law-abiding employer; they are special situations. Refusal to bargain and discrimination against an employee to discourage membership in a union are unfair labor practices of major importance to the higher management of a company but are only rarely committed by the supervisor. He can contribute to a refusal to bargain, though, and perhaps cause the union to be installed even though it has not won an election by accepting, examining, or even touching authorization cards or other evidence of a union's majority. This is perhaps exaggerated, but where a company or supervisor knows that a majority of the employees have appointed a union, it is obliged to bargain with that union, with or without an election. **Examining any type of union proof of a majority is an urgent "don't", an act which must not be performed under any circumstances.**

He may also be responsible for the "discrimination" violation, if he takes it on himself to punish union supporters by ending their employment, giving them bad assignments, or by isolating them, though in the same job and grade. Most supervisors would know not to do any of these by using common sense; it is in the area of "interference" that common sense is not enough. The supervisor must inform himself of the specifics.

". . . To interfere with, restrain or coerce employees in the exercise of their right . . .", then, is the supervisor's ball park. The details are many and it is this proliferation of detail that clogs the brain passages and often reduces what should be the aggressive key man in the campaign to a state of frustrated withdrawal.

These details include actually interfering with organization by forbidding employees to solicit others on non-working time or distributing literature in non-working areas, threatening employees with adverse employer action if the union wins, or threatening actual physical violence. Questioning employees about their union activities or preferences is unlawful but otherwise gaining this information through employee contacts is not unlawful and is an essential responsibility of the supervisor. Questioning itself may not be unlawful unless its purpose is to take reprisals against someone for his union activity, but the supervisor would be well advised to get the okay of management before he does *any* questioning about union activity. Removing privileges or threatening to remove them, in order to discourage union activity is considered interference. Spying on union activity or open surveillance of their meetings and their doings will nearly always be ruled interference.

This sounds very imposing indeed and it is not a complete list. But most of the things that supervisors do that lead to the unfair labor practice hearings we find in the records are not accidental or unwitting happenings. They are usually in situations where the employer has set out to defeat the union with every means at his disposal and with little thought for the law. These cases are rare, unnecessary and unwise, because the employer who wins an election by threatening his people and otherwise taking unfair advantage of them will have to live with a sullen, resentful work force.

The supervisor who tries to do the right thing should not feel unduly restricted by these laws and interpretations because a) minor technical violations are usually ruled okay unless they are part of a larger pattern of illegal conduct by the company, b) the remedy for nearly all of the unlawful acts that a supervisor can commit is generally no more than a rerun of the election and the posting of a notice, and c) in most instances a charge will never be filed, particularly where the losing union decides it can do no better in a new election.

Board Election Rules

There is another set of restrictions on supervisor conduct that is set forth not in the law, but in the procedures and regulations of the NLRB. This is a long list of activities, most of them resembling the interference unfair labor practice, that upset what the Board calls the "laboratory atmosphere" it believes should surround its elections. They are not violations of federal law. The only remedy for these violations, alone, is to rerun the election.

Some supervisor actions that may tend to destroy this atmosphere are calling an employee to his office or "seat of authority" to talk to him about unionism (though the conversation itself may be completely lawful); making a speech (an otherwise lawful one) to an assembled group of employees on company time, a "captive" audience, within twenty-four hours of the election; injecting the racial issues to an extent that goes beyond the boundaries of truthful information needed by the employee to make a reasoned choice; making home visits to discuss union matters; and emphasizing too heavily the possible economic consequences of having a union in the plant. All in all, it is a potpourri of actions that, in the Board's words, might tend to "create an atmosphere of fear and confusion." Employer statements that are found to be unlawful interference with employee rights will usually be found also to be interference with the election process. But the key point to remember is that a statement, though *not* an unfair labor practice which breaks the law, may still be grounds for setting an election aside and ordering a new one.

Another regulation of the Board, not a specific provision of the Act, that has great impact on the supervisor is the *Excelsior* rule that requires an employer to supply the Board with a list of the names and addresses of all the employees in the proposed bargaining unit, for delivery to the organizing union. This gives the union the ability to make house calls as its time and resources permit and to make mass mailings without having to put together a list of addresses volunteered by cooperating employees. How does this affect the supervisor? It puts maximum pressure on him to learn from his face-to-face contacts with employees the tenor and thrust of the union's campaign and to counter rumors, half-truths and lies that are planted in home calls. He must also work to overcome the great personal pressures and racial issues that can be brought to bear in the privacy of employees' homes.

The *Excelsior* rule puts a premium on successfully resisting the union's first drive to gather enough authorization cards to support a petition for an election, since the rule does not come into play until the union can demonstrate to the NLRB a "show of interest" by 30% of the employees.

Authorization Cards Honored

A recent trend of NLRB thought has changed all of the rules of organizing and, for the employer, the whole tenor of the resistance. This is the Board's increasing reliance on the authorization card to establish a union's majority status. This had been a routine method in the days prior to the Taft-Hartley amendments to the old Wagner Act, but in those amendments it was spelled out that a secret ballot election was to be the sole method the NLRB could use to certify a union as majority representative. Presumably the cards were to be useful only for determining whether there was a show of interest in the union.

The Board has returned to the use of authorization cards by ruling that an employer who accepts this evidence of a majority is obliged to bargain with the union. The company is not obliged to examine evidence of this sort, however. Authorization cards are used also as a basis for ordering the company to bargain with a union even after a union loss, when, in the Board's opinion, the company's serious unfair labor practices tend to preclude a later fair election. Unfair labor practices serious enough to call for a bargaining order occur, for example, when a manager questions employees about their union activities and their contacts with NLRB agents and threatens to withdraw certain benefits if the plant becomes unionized.

The great change in the company's strategy of resistance, then, is the shifting of major emphasis toward preventing the union's getting a majority of the employees signed up on cards. Many of the cards are solicited in that phase of the union's drive when it is still working "underground", has not yet come to the gates in open solicitation and handbilling. The supervisor is the prime gatherer of information in this phase. When the card-gathering is in the open, he also must communicate to employees the fact that these cards they are asked to sign are not merely requests for an election, as the union often implies, but may be shown to the company to get the union declared the bargaining agent.

Pre-Drive Actions

Before the union organizing campaign begins, there are many things a company can do to help maintain its union-free status. The supervisor is almost unlimited by the law in the actions he can take in these times. He should be alert to dissatisfying factors in the work situation, whether physical facilities or interpersonal frictions and grievances; he should be identifying workmen who perennially sow dissatisfaction, establishing and keeping open his channels of communication with his workers, building credibility and deliberately cultivating sources of information that will give early warning of a union's presence. He should carefully identify the informal leaders among his work group and create rapport with them. He must be careful not to create, accidentally, craft lines in the work group that may enable a union to "carve out" a small group for organization. He should make it clear to those under his supervision that the company prefers to operate without a union.

The Undercover Campaign

When the first or undercover phase of the union's organizing drive begins, there is still a great deal the supervisor can do without running afoul of the law. He gathers information and, if management chooses, will oppose the union's attempt to secure authorization cards. The unfair labor practices must be watched now, especially questioning employees and discriminating against pro-union people.

The Open Campaign

The second phase, when the union's drive is out in the open, but no demand for recognition has been made on the company or an election petition filed, increases the risk of unfair labor practices for a company, since it is now on notice that the union is active. In some instances the union will send a registered letter listing the names of its principal employee supporters, to get them the full protection of the law.

When a petition for an election has been filed with the NLRB, all the Board's election rules arise to further modify the behavior of the supervisor. Nonetheless he must be even more active in this third phase, countering union propaganda, evaluating the pro-company feelings of each of his people to keep correctly informed on the progress of the union's campaign and identifying the key issues of the campaign. He should recommend company action to meet these issues.

The Law's View

Most of this discussion seems to reinforce the self-defeating behavior of emphasizing "don'ts". To speak effectively, the supervisor needs a concept of how the law views his employees, whom he knows as dignified human souls, self-reliant, fun-loving people. The law looks at these people as if they were harried, gullible individuals living always in fear that something will happen to disturb their fingertip hold on the job. A job on which they are deemed desperately dependent. The NLRB goes further, seemingly, to make the assumption that something is amiss when employees vote against a union. An example of the NLRB view of the employees' intellectual capacity is its declaring the showing of a movie, *And Women Must Weep*, an upset of its election process, on the basis that it was not an exact rendition of the situation it was based on. To assume that people who have been exposed to movie documentaries, advertising and propaganda all their lives are unable to comprehend the difference between a movie and the real world is to credit them with minimum brain power.

There are many themes the supervisor can pursue in communicating with his people. He can give critical opinions of unions, union leaders and union policies. He can inform employees of known communists, racketeering or other undesirable elements active in the union. He can emphasize to his people that they are not obliged to vote for the union even though they had signed an authorization card. He can inform his people that the company would rather deal direct with them rather than through a third party, the union. He can tell his people that unionization will disrupt easy-going employee-employer relationships. He can inform employees how their wages and benefits compare with union firms where they are less desirable. He can inform employees that the law permits hiring a replacement for any employee who is on a strike for economic reasons. He can inform employees of any untrue or misleading statements made by the union in its propaganda and get the correct facts to them. He can inform the employees if there is reason to believe the local union will be dominated by the international union and they will have little voice in its operation. He can inform employees of all the disadvantages of belonging to a union such as paying dues, fines and assessments, the possibility of strikes and serving in a picket line.

The supervisor need not sacrifice efficiency or be pushed around because the organizers are busy. He can enforce plant rules impartially, regardless of an employee's support of a union. He can put outside organizers off company premises, in most situations. He can insist that employee solicitation or discussion of union activities be conducted outside of working time.

A General Rule

More important, though, a supervisor needs to move from a mass of memorized tabus to a general rule of positive conduct. A working rule may be synthesized from all the "do's" and "don'ts": *The supervisor cannot use the unique power of his position to influence employees' choice of a representative.* Note he can use all his personal prestige and power; he just cannot throw around the weight of the company's influence on the employees' lives, using his position of authority.

Another approach the supervisor can take toward accomplishing his purpose is to adopt the frame of mind that he is giving his employees all the information they need on which to base a "no union" vote. He is not forcing them to vote a certain way; but neither is he pretending to present both sides of the question. They don't expect him to; he will seem wishy-washy. They are already hearing the other side.

The possibilities for communicating forcefully and legally are almost endless.

In summary, in labor law a person's being a "supervisor" is not just a state of mind or a title, but a clearly defined condition based on the work he performs. The supervisor is the pivotal person in the company's resistance to the union organizer. He must not boggle at the law's and the NLRB's demands on his communication skills. Though the supervisor is subject to being required to take the part of the company, he should carry this responsibility enthusiastically and not just because his company will be more secure. The fact is he stands to benefit most from the union-free life, because he will continue to have the authority to match his basic responsibility for getting things done through his people, in an atmosphere of teamwork and mutual confidence.

Conclusion

After a hectic period of time in which a union has explored the ground, staged a sub rosa campaign, conducted a full-scale open organizing drive and then suffered defeat in an NLRB election, the company may send one last letter to all employees.

Though successful, the management must not leave a bitter taste after a NO UNION vote by suddenly cutting off communications. The path must be cleared for the good feelings and sound relations that will continue to repel hopeful organizers:

> The results of the election held in the plant two weeks ago have now been certified by the National Labor Relations Board.
>
> This document of certification, which officially solves the problem that has been before us, brought home to me, again, the great interest in Superior's future you showed by your almost unanimous participation.
>
> I firmly believe your interest was justified, since your vote in favor of Superior's way of operating is certain to have a lasting effect on our stability. We will now be able to move forward together to more security and better personal relations than we have ever had. The campaign has shown us clearly some human mistakes we have made and we are moving to correct them.
>
> I should like to add my thanks for the attention you gave our letters and talks in the time before the election.
>
> All of us in management and supervision are gratified, too, that there is no longer unrest or confusion to be found in the

plant, in spite of the trying weeks we have seen. My earnest hope is that we will continue to take all our problems in stride, with this same spirit of teamwork and good fellowship.

Sincerely,

At a time like this a supervisor is keenly aware of the things he could have done better had he been better prepared. The supervisor who has not been through such a union organizing attempt will not find it easy to know what he should be doing to prepare himself for the challenging task of union-free supervision.

Rarely does a company win without supervisors who are prepared. The union-free supervisor must have, first of all, the *desire* to continue without a union taking a position between himself and his men. Secondly, he must know what needs doing and what he must do to be prepared. Finally, he must understand that the time to act, to get himself where he wants to be, is *now*.

The well-run union, the one most likely to win an election, will not invest the talent of its organizers in a work group that is motivated to work, that holds its management in high regard, *and whose supervision is prepared to defend against the union campaign*. This kind of a union will learn of these facts and an election will not take place.

Knowing the impact of unionism on his own job situation, on his employees and on his company will give a supervisor the desire he needs. Knowing how a union organizes and how a company resists gives him a background of knowledge on which to prepare himself.

The next step is realizing that the real key is the individual employee, not only as he stands in the voting booth with a ballot in his hand, but as he fences verbally with a union organizer in the parlor of his home or in a bull session with other employees during a break at work.

And beyond this, the supervisor must realize that to influence this employee he must use all the tools that are available to the supervisor today. He must establish that easy relationship that is so vital in full two-way communication.

How he communicates is not nearly so important as *what*. He must put over to his people that he and the rest of management expect the worker's best: not just a hand, but a whole man, with a talent to think and create. He must be saying, in deed as well as word, that the boss will support each person in reaching his job goals and his on-the-job personal goals.

Index

Alliance for Labor Action, 24
American Institute of Chemical Engineers, 78
"And Women Must Weep", 210
Appraisal factors, supervisory, 156
Associations, professional, 78
Authorization cards, 27, 28, 208
Autocratic leadership, 70

Bargaining unit, determination of, 68, 77
Barkin, Solomon, 138
Beeler, Duane, 18
Bulletin boards, 190-191
Business climate, 40

Camera, supervisor's use of, 190
Cape Canaveral, 15
Captive audience 101, 110, 130-133
Card check, 21
"Carve out", 46
"Cell" of sympathizers, 26
Chamber of Commerce, 23

Charisma, 169-170
Checkoff of dues, 36
"Company union", 191
Complaints, 51
Concern orientation, 185
Conglomerates, 96
Consent election, 32
Contracting work out, 5, 9
Coverage under LMRA, 77

Daily Plan, 189
Demand for recognition, 30
Democratic leadership, 170
Department of Labor, 139
Discipline, 11, 51, 167-169
Disclaimer of interest, 32
Dues, 13

Election rules, 207
Electrical Workers, 76
Employer election petition, 67
Equal Employment Opportunities Commission, 15
Equal Employment Opportunity, 11, 15, 42
"Excelsior" rule, 33, 207
Exploratory phase, 22

Fair Labor Standards Act, 11, 53, 77, 84
Featherbedding, 4, 10, 14
Fence-mending, 63, 65
Fines by union, 6, 13
Flexible hours, 53
Fortune Cookies, 71
Free rider, 90

Game of work, the, 142, 143

Government regulation, effect on nompany, 5
Grid, management, 161
Grievances, 7, 51, 198
  log, 199
  plan, 199

Hard-core unemployed, 139
Health plans, 49
Herzberg, Frederick, 143, 145
Holdover, 51
"How to Be a More Effective Union Representative," 18
Huff, Sam, 148

"Invasion" technique, 30

James, William, 143
Job action, 89
Job enrichment, 196
Jurisdictional stride, 122
Jurisdiction, union, 4

Kurshenbaum, Harry, 18

LM-1, LM-2, LM-30, 42
Labor Department, 139
Labor-Management Relations Act, 203-204
Labor Organization Annual Report, 42
Labor Organization Information Report, 42
Laissez-faire leadership, 170
Law, effect on company, 5
Layoffs, 51
Leadership style, 161-163

Long range company program, 40-59, 61, 82-84, 89
Longshoremen, 10

"Make work", 10
Management grid, 161
Management rights, 9-11
Man study, 163-164
Marine Engineers Benevolent Association, 78
Medical plans, 49
Merchant marine, 16
Mine Workers, 76
Motivator-dissatisfier theory, 145-147

National Labor Relations Board (see NLRB)
National Society of Professional Engineers, 78
NLRB, 7, 14, 17, 21, 41, 42, 45, 59, 63, 65-69, 203, 210
NLRB Election Report, 42

Ombudsman, 191-192
Overtime, 9
   rotation of, 197

Part-time work, 54
Pay envelope stuffers, 71
Pension plans, 50
"People Book", 187
Performance review, 196
Post-election actions, 73, 74
Pre-drive actions of supervisor, 208
Professional associations, 78
Professional societies, 78

Questionnaire behavior, 144

Recorder, 190
Riesel, Victor, 15
Right to work, 36
Rules, work, 4

Savings plans, 50
Secondary strike, 122
Security, 6
Seniority, 7, 9, 50
Shift schedules, 54
Short range company program, 61-74, 85-87, 92-93
Short work week, 53
Sick pay, 49
"Six Sins", 160
Societies, professional, 78
Solicitation rules, 46
Strikes, 7, 67, 122
Style, leadership, 161
Sub rosa campaign, 4, 24, 62, 67
Successor clause, 91
Superseniority, 120
Supervisor traits, 157, 158
Supervisory appraisal factors, 156
Supervisory skills, areas of, 155
Sweetheart contract, 35
Sympathy strike, 121

Taft-Hartley Act, 208
Task force, 61
Teamsters, 76
Technicians, 80, 114
Technological change clause, 96
Textile Workers of America, 138
Time clock, 53
Trade secrets, 11
Traits of supervisors, 158
"Truth Forum", 72, 73

Unfair labor practices, 203, 205-206
Unionism, impact of
  on company, 5
  on employee, 11
  on nation, 14
  on supervisor, 16

Wages, 48
Wagner Act, 208
Whipsaw strike, 122
Work simplification, 198
Workmen's Compensation, 40